The Nella Novella

Lessons Earned on a Sensually Raw Journey

Through Love, Desire, and Self-Discovery

By Nella Novella

THE NELLA NOVELLA
Copyright © 2025 by Northern Lights Publishing

All rights reserved. No part of this book may be used or reproduced in any manner whatsoever without written permission of the copyright holder, except in the case of brief quotations in critical articles and reviews. For more information, contact: thenellanovella@gmail.com

Design & Production: Domini Dragoone/Sage Folio Creative
Cover photo: © Александра Кумелан/Pexels

ISBN (paperback): 979-8-9925511-0-5
ISBN (e-book): 979-8-9925511-1-2

Printed in the United States of America

This book is a memoir. It reflects the author's present recollections of experiences over time. It contains descriptions of intimate encounters and includes explicit discussions of sex and drug use, which may be triggering or distressing to some readers. The author acknowledges that these topics can be deeply sensitive and may evoke strong emotional responses. Names and characteristics have been changed throughout to protect the privacy of the individuals, some events have been compressed, and some dialogue has been recreated. All individuals portrayed are consenting and of a similar age, unless otherwise noted.

Contents

Dear Reader 1
Cherry Popper 4
Virgin Boy 11
Altar Adonis 16
First Boyfriend 19
Two-Inch Boy 25
Bam Bam 28
Buddy 32
Lord Farquaad 35
Lip Lad 38
Spiky-Hair Dude 42
Wannabe Gangster 45
Final Revenge Boy 48
My Fingers 51
Mr. BBQ 53
GBF 56
Pedro 60

Parking Prince	66
Tattoo Ninja	72
LOML	77
The Italian	86
Disco Dan	91
Russian Boy	96
Tinder Boo	100
Fortunate Fella	108
Drive-By Guy	113
Cloud-Snatcher	116
Flash	122
Bar Master	125
Girlfriend	129
Captain Try Too Hard	133
McDreamy	137
Blondie	142
Mac Daddy and Bombshell	146
Bullet Bill	154
Bootyhole Bandit	160
Euro Lover	164
New York	172
Dud	178
Massage Man	188
Aladdin	194
Myself	215

Dear Reader,

———

I want to prepare you for what is about to come. Hopefully you come too. But from better circumstances than some of mine.

I never imagined I'd be writing about sex—especially if you asked my younger self about the subject. Back then, I was the ultimate tomboy. Flirting for me meant beating the boys in arm wrestling and knocking the wind out of them with my impressive punch. My hair was always in a ponytail, and I lived in baggy clothes. Comfort and mobility were my top priorities—after all, you never knew when someone might challenge you to a spontaneous race or a showdown of athletic prowess. But then came the summer before eighth grade, and let's just say, everything took a very unexpected turn!

While chatting about a massive crush I had with one of my guy friends, he gave me some advice: If I wanted him (or any guy, really) to notice me, I'd have to retire my loose-fitting clothing, style my pulled-back hair, and "be more girly."

I had romance in my heart and wanted to be desired, so I changed.

I straightened my hair with a clothing iron—because back then, hair straighteners were basically a luxury for the rich—and cat-walked into the first day of school in a miniskirt and cleavage-hugging top that turned every boy's head in the schoolyard. They had never seen or imagined me like this. It was exhilarating. I reveled in the newfound attention.

The feelings were short-lived when soon after, a rumor was spread that I gave someone a blowjob. I was mortified. All I wanted was to hold hands with the guy I liked; I hadn't even had my first kiss yet! Instead, I found myself labeled a whore for something I hadn't done. Even my so-called friends joined in on the gossip. What I thought would be my upcoming year of the new me quickly spiraled into the opposite. My young mind was relentlessly tormented.

I couldn't stand the thought of facing the same people in high school who loudly whispered about me in the hallways. So, I decided to start fresh at a school where no one knew my past. To my disappointment, the boys there mocked me for being a virgin. It was an endless cycle of pressure and shame, leading me to suppress my sexual feelings for fear of ridicule.

I would eventually learn, however, that suppressing emotions only made them stronger.

I realized I wasn't meant to live in a place of limitation, especially when it came to my thoughts and desires. I liberated myself from the constraints of judgment and embraced my true self with naked authenticity. I was ready to love whoever I wanted, wherever I wanted, and however I wanted!

So here it is, the good, bad, terrible, cringy, awkward, funny, and steamy confessions of a sex-venturous girl growing into herself.

Cherry Popper

My childhood was typical for a middle-class girl: a hard-working mom, a part-time dad, more than a few questionable friends, and a head full of delusions of Disney grandeur. I was convinced my Prince Charming would soon arrive to whisk me away from this non-fairy-tale life.

Spoiler alert: That never happened. Not even close.

My first time came during a tropical family vacation that I hadn't even wanted to be part of. At fifteen, I was repulsed by the idea of playing resort games with people three times my age. So, I escaped to an empty basketball court to vent my teenage frustrations. I figured it might be the perfect spot to meet some boys.

Just ten minutes into my intense one-on-one with myself, I locked eyes with a handsome young fellow walking by. It was more than just a passing glance—so I knew the love-gods heard my prayers. My heart skipped a beat as he leaned against the fence, clearly focused on watching me. Surprising even myself with my boldness, I stopped shooting hoops and walked straight up to him. I knew I couldn't let this opportunity pass; I was ready for my true love. I started dreaming of our life together—only to have my vision shattered when I discovered he didn't speak a word of English.

Disappointed was an understatement.

As I watched him struggle to communicate, I refused to accept defeat so easily. He had to be my prince, and I would do everything in my power to make it work.

I gestured to the ball and the hoop, asking him in made-up sign language to play basketball with me. After all, sports were pretty universal, right? He hopped the fence and followed me to the court.

Our game started off friendly as we felt out each others' abilities, but then, out of nowhere, he dunked on me! Not once, not twice, but probably five times. I transformed into a new person. My vision narrowed. Nothing was going to stop me from kicking his ass. When he hung off the rim for the sixth time, I body-slammed him so hard that he lost his balance on the way down, hitting the ground with a big thud. I stood over him triumphantly, holding the ball while he clutched his ankle!

I didn't think it was that serious until he got up to walk and could only manage a hobble. My triumph faded fast when I realized I'd hurt the only friend I had on this boring family vacation. At five-two and skinny, I never imagined I could injure someone who towered over me in height and weight. Guess I had superhuman little-person strength!

As I apologized over and over, he took my hand and led me away. It couldn't be that bad if he wanted to hold hands, right? This was my first taste of romance, and my heart was bursting. Even if we didn't speak the same language, this had to be the beginning of my happy ending.

We spent the rest of the day together, hand in hand, visiting all his friends around the resort. None of them spoke English, so there I was like the Mona Lisa—smiling and observing as if I belonged. It was 2004, and there were no smartphones to scroll through during awkward moments. I figured he'd do the same for me when I introduced him to my friends, so I didn't mind. Anything for love, right?

Our hand-holding turned into passionate kisses when he led me to a secluded place on the beach. To me, it felt like he had waited a lifetime to taste my lips. I felt the same. The ocean serenaded us as our tongues moved in harmony. It was perfect.

There was nothing that could stop this fairytale from happening, language barrier or not. We would overcome anything!

I woke up bright and early the next morning, bursting with excitement to spend another day with the love of my life. With a bounce in my step, I set out to find him, certain it wouldn't take long for us to reunite. Then I turned the corner—and there he was, sitting at the bar with a cast that stretched from his toes to his hip. I was shocked. Here I was thinking he was being dramatic with all the hobbling he was doing so he could savor the moments he had with me, but he was genuinely hurt.

All I could do was awkwardly walk over to him, unsure of how he would feel. But my doubts vanished the moment he pulled me in to say hello with his lips. I couldn't believe he still wanted me! My heart soared with happiness.

The second day was even better than the first. There was nothing for us to do but kiss and stare deeply into each other's eyes. I never wanted this unspoken, passionate story to end. He took me to the internet café and introduced me to his only English-speaking friend who couldn't believe we'd spent two days together without understanding a word. I smiled because you don't need to speak the same language when you're talking with your soul, right? We used Google Translate for our first real conversation, and when he told me I was beautiful in English, I was completely smitten.

We ended our second day on a hammock together by the beach. We both wanted to do more than kiss, but unfortunately, it was the last day of my period. I looked like a wild woman doing a rain dance as I tried to explain it to him with arm movements and hand gestures. But he was not picking up what I was putting down. So we made out for another twenty minutes while he attempted to push his finger past the tampon inside of me. His confused and frustrated breaths made me laugh. I finally grabbed his hand and told him "tomorrow." I didn't think he understood, but I wasn't worried about it. I knew we would laugh about it when we learned each other's languages.

I woke up early the next day, eager to find my beautiful limping boy. I had made up my mind—today, I would lose my virginity. Nothing else mattered but us. I started my search at the bars and then combed through every inch of the resort as the day turned to night, but he was nowhere to be found! I figured we must have just kept missing each other, so my search continued for the next three days. He had vanished without a trace. I was so confused.

On my final day, desperate to see him one last time before heading home, I convinced his English-speaking friend from the internet café to help me track him down. There had to be a logical reason for his disappearance. I was sure he cared about me.

His friend took me to his house across the street from the resort, but it was completely empty—no furniture, people, or signs of life. I couldn't hide my bewilderment when the neighbor informed us that he had moved. I was crushed!

This asshole couldn't think to draw a pictogram or something to let me know that I was never going to see him again? I truly believed I had found my soulmate. How could he do this? All our beautiful moments flashed through my mind as the painful realization hit: He had played me.

I always knew I didn't want my first time to be with someone I cared about—this was a perfect example why. Most young boys left a trail of broken hearts, sticking their penis into anything that gave them attention. I had lost count of how many times I had consoled girlfriends over this same situation. I didn't want my story to end up the same way, nor did I want to become a forty-year-old virgin. So, I thanked the universe for removing Broken Foot Boy from my life and decided to fuck his friend.

Cherry Popper knew everyone at the resort, which enabled our access to an empty, just-cleaned room. Moonlight through the window lit the space enough to make the space borderline romantic. I turned to him and almost hit him in the nose when I jumped up on my tippy toes to kiss him. He was tall, and I was awkwardly nervous. I pulled him onto the bed after we'd uncomfortably stand-kissed for a moment, wondering why he wasn't taking the initiative. It was not his first time, and the only reference I had for what we were about to do was the love scene in the *Titanic* movie.

I rushed to take my clothes off and watched him do the same. Then, for the first time, I saw it. A penis. It bobbed like a charmed snake right before he guided it to its destination. "*Ah,* it's alive," my brain whispered as I lay back.

He knew it was my first time, so he eased inside gently. Before I could think twice I threw him off of me with a yelp, sending him crashing into the nightstand as I breathed in the pain of my hymen breaking. Though I knew this could happen, thanks to a sex ed class in school, my reflexes didn't think. They just "reflexed." I held my breath as I looked at him sprawled across the floor. Thankfully he was okay. I didn't have to add another broken limb to my collection of souvenirs for the trip.

We continued where we left off. All I could remember thinking was *Is this it?* until he finished. It felt like a chore that needed choring.

There you have it. Numero uno. Painful. Not romantic or exciting. And definitely not my Prince Charming. It was perfect. I would never have to see him again or worry about him spreading the news to the world like the loudmouthed immature boys I knew back home. I felt powerful and unattached as I boarded the plane the next day.

I was still a little bummed about Broken Foot Boy ghosting me until I received an email from him demanding that I send him some money and a cell phone. Jerk.

Lesson one: Disney lies. You may get a happy ending, but it will end up being more like a sitcom than a fairy tale.

Virgin Boy

Virgin Boy was the result of my virgin liver attempting to process five Long Island iced teas.

It was the summer before eleventh grade, and I felt like a caged bird. My mother's strictness loomed over me. I had no one to help me escape my home troubles. I had introduced my best friend to my childhood friends, only to have them all subsequently ditch me for each other. I was an angry mess inside. The idea of returning to a school full of people I despised only fueled my resentment, so I made the bold choice to move in with my father. He lived in a small town eight hours away from everything I had ever known.

As I boarded the bus to my new life, tears streamed down my face, an unfamiliar sensation. I had come to view crying as a sign of weakness, having been hardened by countless social situations that taught me that I couldn't express myself. I waved goodbye to my mom as she mirrored my feelings through the window. Deep down, we both knew this was for the best.

Starting over in the ninth grade made it easier for me to do it again in the eleventh, and though this was a much bigger move, I felt aligned with my decision. I was excited for this adventure.

During the first couple of months, my social life went as anticipated. Minimal. I knew it would take time to build relationships, so I wasn't concerned that my only friend was my high school dropout neighbor. All the other kids resided on the opposite side of my sidewalk-less town. Without a car, seeing them was impossible; so I took whatever company I could get.

It was a typical boring night in her grungy room with her younger unstimulating male cousin. While we were figuring out what to do, a gentleman caller swept her away for a romp. She took her position as the neighborhood call girl very seriously. I didn't judge.

I found myself stuck with her cousin, who just didn't spark any interest in me. I was completely bored and had to get out of there. With few friends and limited funds, my only option for escape was a persistent older suitor who came with a car. We'd met a week earlier when he supplied me and my girlfriend with our first cocaine experience. I wasn't soberly attracted to him but didn't mind when he pulled my mouth to his after the copious number of shots and monster lines that my newbie self had no business doing. He had been blowing up my phone ever since so I knew he would rescue me if asked. He was over five minutes after I called.

It was 7 p.m., and we decided to hit up a local restaurant/bar for some appetizers—because in a small town, this was all there was to do (aside from drugs). I made sure to drag the cousin along so the older suitor would keep his grabby gremlin alter ego in check. I knew after one night with him that he was a sloppy alcoholic.

As soon as we stepped inside, Gremlin Guy wasted no time grabbing a Long Island iced tea. I was starving and definitely not in the mood to deal with a reckless drunk driver. Once we settled at our table, I quickly seized his drink and polished it off. "For the safety of the collective!" I declared. He and my liver weren't very happy, especially after my fifth confiscated drink. But I didn't care. I wasn't about to die in a drunk-driving accident just because I was bored.

By the time we returned to my friend's room, I was pretty intoxicated. My friend still hadn't come back, and Gremlin Guy stormed off in a huff when I turned down his advances for a kiss. So there I was again, stuck with the ever-uninteresting cousin.

We plopped down in front of the TV as I felt the alcohol course through me. I was itching for something—anything—exciting. Suddenly, I felt all these suppressed desires crawling up from a mysterious place deep within. I harbored no feelings for the boy next to me, and we both knew I was way out of his league. But I wanted to feel a dick inside of me, and so I decided he would have to do.

I looked him dead in the face and asked if he would like to have sex. He sat there quietly before confessing that he had never done it before. I told him about my first experience, reassuring him that we were both in the same awkward boat. "Okay," he said with a nod, then excused himself to the bathroom for what I can only assume was a pep talk. When he came back I could see his boner through his pants. I liked that he was ready.

I fumbled to take his clothes off while pulling him on top of me. Even in my drunken state I knew this was very unsexy. I wasn't familiar with foreplay and had no desire to kiss him. I put the condom on like my sex ed class taught me and pulled him close so he could get it in. He thumped his body repeatedly against mine as I tried to figure out why wanting it felt better than having it. Wasn't sex supposed to be pleasurable? Why did everyone rave about this?

I decided that maybe if I had control it would feel better, so I ordered him onto his back. When I hopped on top I realized I had no idea how to be there. I squirmed around trying to figure out how to bounce like the woman in the only porno I'd ever watched. I felt like a hippo. This was not as glamorous and empowering as I imagined. I was glad the phone rang because I had lost my desire, and he had lost his erection. We promised not to tell anyone, and I left drunk and unsatisfied.

The next week I heard him bragging about the experience to a group of friends at school. I was furious but not surprised. I pretended not to know him for the rest of my life.

Many people will promise the world,
but few will honor their word.

Altar Adonis

I first laid eyes on Altar Adonis in middle school when he became the newly appointed altar server at the Sunday church service my family religiously attended. He stood tall, with hair that looked more perfect than any of my holy intentions and eyes that could make a nun blush. After two weeks of devout admiration, my twelve-year-old self could worship him from afar no longer. So I became an altar girl—I had to sit right beside him.

After I signed up, he handed me a paper with his number and said to call if I had any questions. Two days later, I compiled a list and dialed him, eager to hear his heavenly voice before seeing him again. Even at a young age, the deep timbre of his tone evoked something within me.

Our friendship blossomed gradually. Though strict rules at my house kept us from hanging out, we connected through marathon phone conversations. He was a year older and a total rebel; his altar server stint was the result of a pizza bribe from his Catholic school. His true persona thrived on the streets, selling drugs and finding different ways to hustle for a dollar. He lived the life my wannabe bad-girl self wanted.

Our phone chats slowed when I went to high school and grew even more sporadic after I'd moved in with my father. But we kept in contact here and there.

During a random conversation when I was seventeen, I expressed how much I missed being at my mom's. To my surprise, I soon received an email with a flight home scheduled for the following weekend. My teenage desire for intimacy was already burning for him; now, it was an inferno. He picked me up from the airport and took me out for a nice dinner. All I had to do was look at him for him to know it was finally time.

Upon arrival at his place, he suggested we play a game of strip darts. I was too excited to even care about any competition and purposely missed my target by a mile to get us both naked faster. He did the same. As our last pieces of clothing were shed, he kissed me softly. Nothing like the deep passion I dreamed about when our lips and bodies intertwined in my fantasies, but I figured it would get better. He laid me down gently and slowly eased himself inside. He was quite large, so it was a little painful, but I wanted it and felt ready. I gasped in excitement as he began to find his rhythm. I thought I was finally going to experience the kind of sex that people raved about. Until he pulled out ten seconds later. I asked if he was alright, and he began to freak out, saying that there was blood. I looked down to see what the issue was and swear I practically needed a magnifying glass to find the tiny drop of blood he was going on about. The fuck? I was still practically a virgin. What did he expect was going to happen with that elephant trunk he had down there? Even my inexperienced self knew this was normal. I put my clothes on as he ripped the sheets off dramatically. How embarrassing. All this build-up through the years for this? After running around like a crazy Muppet, he summoned me back to his newly made bed. I lay beside him wide-eyed as he held me tight and fell asleep. Before I even had a second to process everything, he started snoring. All my fantasies of him were in shambles. He went from Altar Adonis to Pew Pal real quick. I snuck out shortly after.

With a little more experience and a second try a couple of years later, I realized Pew Pal was a two-pump chump. Also known as a premature ejaculator. He humiliated me so deeply that I was blinded to the fact that he was embarrassed of himself. So rude! At least I got a free flight out of it.

Those who make you feel
self-conscious are often just
projecting their own insecurities.

First Boyfriend

I met my First Boyfriend in the ancient era of MySpace. After catching sight of him in a photo with a mutual friend, I knew he had to be mine. He looked like the quintessential neighborhood bad boy, radiating an allure impossible to resist. With his sun-kissed skin and dark features, he held a direct line to my heart. The missing piece I was sure I was looking for.

Our relationship was made official a mere week after our first hangout, and I was head over heels. He seemed flawless, save for a couple of character quirks I was sure I could "fix." Bless my naïve seventeen-year-old heart.

First Boyfriend's concept of a good time was smoking to obliteration with his homies—every single day. This boy found more joy in reveling in a haze of weed than a squirrel did collecting nuts. Though fun to participate in at first, I quickly realized it was far from my scene. I was on the brink of graduating high school and bursting with visions of a vibrant future in the real world. I craved nice things and dreamed of globe-trotting adventures. I couldn't check off my bucket list with a bum who spent the minimal money he had on getting high.

I dove into the first item on my "making my ideal boyfriend" checklist—with the ultimatum that he get a job. I figured he would be less fixated on smoking weed all day if he had something more fulfilling to occupy his time with. My unique method of persuasion was to withhold sex until his first day of work, convinced that would light a fire under him. Little did I know I was about to get a PhD in "Misjudging the Motivational Power of Withholding Sex."

The first three months of our relationship were stuck at first base with no sign of movement. This broke boy refused to look for a job. I was baffled—didn't the male instinct drive them to do anything for a chance at getting laid?

Clearly, I had a lot to learn. As the third month rolled to a close, I grew restless and could wait no longer. I had to take matters into my own hands before I caved and slept with him against my word. So, I marched into the nearest restaurant to his place and sweet-talked the owners into hiring him. They agreed, but only if I worked there too. Problem solved.

He excitedly looked at me after our first shift together and asked if we could finally do it. Um, yes, yes, and more yes! I obviously wanted it more than him. We proceeded to the bathroom, the only room in his ghetto house that wasn't occupied. We made out as our pants came off for the first time together. I could feel our hearts beat in sync. He lifted me shakily off the ground with his muscle-less arms as I wrapped my legs around him. This was the position he knew I fantasized about, so he was gifting it to me for our first time. I was charmed that he remembered this from a conversation months prior. I held onto his neck tightly as he slid inside. He struggled to thrust and hold me as I struggled even more to keep my hands locked around his neck. We were both failing miserably. It did not feel sexy. Finally, he heaved me onto the counter where the sink was and continued giving it to me as I tried not to bang my head into the mirror behind me. He finished shortly in a non-climactic way and asked if I had done the same. That was a no. I had no idea what an orgasm felt like but knew this mechanical tango had failed to get the job done.

The position had looked so much more satisfying in porn. Everything did actually. I was now convinced that my whole idea of sex was wrong. I thought it would be better with someone you loved, but it felt as underwhelming as the first three misadventures.

As we exited the bathroom, I could see he also had something weighing on him. When I finally convinced him to speak up, he admitted that he thought I would feel like a virgin down there because I'd only slept with three people prior. I almost slapped him. This boy had a lot of nerve making a comment like that with a pecker two inches smaller than he'd advertised.

He immediately apologized when he realized how much of a moron he sounded like. I liked that he owned up to his mistakes and forgave him quickly. Besides, I couldn't un-love the person I planned to spend the rest of my life with for something so minuscule. Love was forgiving, right?

Navigating through our sexuality together was exciting. We were both novice lovers, so we made it our thing to try everything in every place with the smallest bit of privacy. Beaches at night, backyards, hallways, the restaurant we worked at together...etc. I liked his little penis and *really* liked his tongue. He gave me my first orgasm with it, which definitely lived up to the hype. I learned quickly that I wasn't able to come through penetration alone. The only way it happened was when my clit was licked. I also learned that sex without foreplay was like going down a waterslide without water. They never taught me that in sex ed.

As our sexual relationship flourished, other aspects declined. He was the center of my universe, but getting high with his friends was the center of his. Jealousy from both sides drove a wedge between us, and we started disagreeing about everything. Our once-in-a-while arguments became more frequent until we broke up every other day. "It doesn't get any better than this" was what our delusional selves always repeated after the mind-blowing make-up sex. We were each other's drug and were both addicted. Codependency at its finest.

I didn't realize our final breakup had happened until it was too late. I was driving to his place, excited to make amends, when I spotted him kissing a mutual friend on his porch. I lost it, slamming my car into park as they ran inside together. Fury coursed through me as I made my way to the door. I was going to beat both of them into another galaxy. They held it closed on the other side as I relentlessly tried to kick it open. The frame shook with every blow but held firm. I could hear them yelling about calling the cops, so I stumbled back to my car, trembling with rage. It was like I had been punched in the gut. I couldn't breathe. I felt like a psycho but didn't know how else to process my heart shattering.

I felt so betrayed. I had never loved anything more than him; we were supposed to be together forever. How could he have moved on so quickly? "Devastated" didn't begin to capture the depth of my pain. This was not how it was meant to go down.

Despite driving past his home every day, desperately hoping for a glimpse of him and calling his phone privately just to hear his voice, I turned down his attempts to reconcile a week later. He wasn't allowed to hurt me like that and get away with it so easily. We needed a substantial break if we ever hoped to have a shot at a future together. Plus, I wanted to explore the penisverse before I settled down.

Predictably, he didn't take my decision very well. Whenever he heard a whisper of me giving another guy attention, he'd leave me voicemails about what a nasty whore I was. He spread rumors about me to anyone who would listen and took it upon himself to steal something from me whenever one of us coerced the other into ex-sex. His disrespect knew no bounds.

Refusing to be a doormat, I resolved to make him pay for every little thing he'd ever said and done. It wasn't revenge—just giving him a taste of his own medicine. All for the hopes that he would shut his stupid face, which I still loved, up and come running back to me apologizing after he recognized the error of his ways. Little did I know, this marked the beginning of my dark downward spiral—a twisted competition to see who could inflict the most pain on the other.

The most dangerous thing about a toxic relationship is believing you can fix it.

Two-Inch Boy

I started my first year of college with an empty bank account, a heart filled with emotional trauma, and no clear direction in my studies. My schedule was packed with the kind of mind-numbing general education courses mandated for a bachelor's degree and a shitty job at a clothing store just to afford them. Life was rough.

My only source of joy was my budding marijuana business. My First Boyfriend taught me the ropes, and all his friends were conveniently my best customers. The perfect scenario for retribution.

I enforced a strict rule: no drugs if my ex was in the vicinity. To buy from me, his friends had to ensure he was nowhere to be seen upon my arrival. This often turned into a drama-filled spectacle that delighted the darkness within me. There was nothing quite like cruising down their street early enough to catch them kicking him to the curb as he threw a bitch fit. I would evil-laugh each time I watched him stomp off.

Two-Inch Boy, the brother of my new supplier, was panty-droppingly gorgeous. I was still too sexually shy to go straight to the "let's just have sex" point, so I planned an evening of partying to get those formalities out of the way.

He sat across the table from me, drinks in hand and smoke curling around us. Every time I glanced his way, I could feel him undressing me with his half-baked eyes. A thrill shot down my spine at the thought of being with a ten-out-of-ten so soon after my breakup. He seemed the perfect rebound.

He followed me to the back of the house when I went to use the restroom. It had been three hours of eye-sex, so I was glad he was taking initiative. He romantically pulled me close when we were out of eyesight from the group and revealed he had a two-inch penis. What the actual fuck? Was this foreplay talk? I was at a loss for words. Did I just set myself up for a night of disappointment? I considered escaping, but he was already leaning in for a kiss. It was too late. I was at the alcohol level of no return anyway. Oh, well.

He led me to his room, where we continued to make out passionately. His experienced self knew exactly what he was doing. Our clothes flew off as every place that needed to be kissed was kissed, and every place that needed to be touched was touched. He even gave attention to areas where I never knew I wanted it. Like my feet. Massaging one gently as he ran his tongue across my toes. He stopped at the big one and focused on sucking the top of it before putting the whole thing in his mouth. It was the strangest, most pleasurable feeling I'd ever experienced. He gave the other toes the same attention before kissing me all the way up to my neck. I was more than ready for the second act.

Thoughts about his lack of length disappeared as he filled me up with his huge (definitely not two-inch) penis. I was so surprised. He knew what he had and how to work it. He pinned me down and gave it to me until my head was banging against the headboard. I didn't care if the whole neighborhood heard. I was in a state of bliss. I almost orgasmed without being eaten out. How could I have gone a whole relationship without experiencing sex as good as this? *Wow!* was all that ran through my mind. Just *wow!*

The next two months were filled with nothing but alcohol and good dick. I've never had so much sex in my life. We couldn't be together for more than ten minutes without being on top of each other. It got to the point where I would run to my car between classes and race to his place for a quickie, even though I was going to sleep over that same evening. But alas, I wasn't about to jump into another relationship. As much as he pleased all my senses, I wanted to meet new penises. Plus, I knew it would take time and inner peace to heal after my breakup. Especially because I was still in love with my ex. I said goodbye to a not-so-happy Two-Inch Boy and took off, pussy first.

If you're not ready to give your heart, don't take someone else's.

Bam Bam

I met Bam Bam the summer before high school through a mutual friend, and within five minutes, he asked if I wanted to make out. I mean, wow—talk about bold! I replied with an unwavering no, though in my head, it was more like "not in this lifetime!" I wasn't attracted to him, and honestly, I was a bit offended that he thought it would be so easy to kiss these lips!

The next day, my girlfriend and I were at the mall when we unexpectedly ran into Bam Bam. Within five minutes, he had pulled me aside and asked me to pose the same question to my friend that he made to me the day before: whether she would make out with him. I was a mix of disbelief and confusion, especially after she agreed and followed him around the corner! I didn't think she was that easy! So there I was, sitting alone for thirty minutes, waiting for her to wrap up her impromptu make-out session. I had finally convinced my mom to let me go to the mall without her chaperoning me, and this was where

I'd ended up. I was so annoyed. The following week, he took her virginity—another plot twist I hadn't seen coming. But hey, good for them!

He wound up attending my high school, and to my surprise, we became decent friends. Even after I moved to my dad's place, we kept in touch with the occasional random text. I knew he'd be a perfect candidate for a new penis experience, so after three years of not seeing him, I decided to call and set up a "hangout." He was totally on board!

We met at the bus stop outside his apartment, and with the rain coming down, I moved in a little closer—just enough to make it known that I wasn't there for small talk. I didn't want to spend five hours beating around the bush. He took the hint and leaned in for a kiss. It felt like I was trying to make out with a dildo attached to the forehead of a mechanical bull. His tongue was fast and hard. Definitely not a candidate for best kisser, but I was sure his tongue would feel nice doing that elsewhere, so I continued.

He took me up to his place. Calling it tiny would have been an understatement. I've seen bathroom stalls with more square footage. It was all of one room with a doll-sized kitchen and bed not meant for anyone over the age of five.

We continued our make-out session as I fumbled my tongue to keep up with the erratic nature of his. He finally stopped (thank god) mid (horrible)-kiss to ask whether we could have sex. Um...what did he think we were going to do in this broom closet?

My positive response caught him off guard. I guess he still remembered my firm *"no"* from five years ago when he asked to make out. Or maybe it was my pretend "hard to get" reputation from high school. I wanted to tell him that I had standards back then to which none of the boys ever measured up. The only reason I was here at present was because I wanted to fuck away my post-breakup sadness with another notch on my penis experience belt. I had no feelings for him in any capacity.

His disco stick was decent-sized and shaped like a banana. I didn't know that some came like that. I was curious to see what it felt like, but as soon as I lay back, he proceeded to ram me like the Energizer Bunny. Bam, bam, bam. Steady and constant, over and over. It was not enjoyable. The condom must've hated it too because at some point it dislodged from his penis and made its way into an unexplored area of my woman parts. Bam Bam was kind enough to fish it out for me after my futile attempts. My sex mood was diminished.

Before I left, we reminisced about our high school days while he cooked me eggs. I couldn't tell whether he shared my mixed feelings about our subpar orgasm-less sexcapade, but it didn't matter—being in his company felt like old times. He walked me downstairs, and we parted with a warm, heartfelt hug. It felt pleasant and mature. He was a true gentleman from beginning to end—a fitting conclusion to an otherwise unsatisfying chapter.

Sexual chemistry is a force you can't force.

Buddy

I met Buddy at the new high school I attended after relocating to my father's place. He was like a male version of me—funny, athletic, mentally stimulating, flirty, and very attractive. A breath of fresh air from the stale roster of boys I grew up with. I was completely captivated.

An undeniable spark crackled between us from the very beginning—one he intentionally fanned without allowing to fully ignite. It was incredibly frustrating. Though he had a girlfriend, he constantly chased me around the halls, trying to kiss me. I wanted to kiss him back—to do everything with him. But I had my "morals," which prioritized others' feelings over my own. I didn't know who his girlfriend was, but either way, I wasn't about to become someone's side chick. That just wasn't my style.

As the years went by, we remained friends, a little less when I had my first boyfriend and a little more immediately after. My ex was extremely jealous of him and our bond. Which, obviously, made me want to fuck him even more.

I subtly hinted at my single status before he picked me up to "catch up and smoke some weed," as I had suggested. It had been a couple of years since we had one-on-one time together.

We pulled into a secluded parking lot near my house while I fumbled through my purse, pretending to search for the lighter we needed to kick off our activities. I didn't want to get high, a fact I knew that he knew. I loved and hated his innate ability to read me. I was still too shy to say it out loud, so I continued rummaging to delay smoke from entering my lungs for as long as possible. My ears turned red with embarrassment as I sensed him reveling in my struggle, waiting and watching for five excruciating minutes before finally suggesting that "we could just have sex instead." YES!

We jumped into the back seat, where we skipped foreplay. I straddled him with most of my clothes still on and started to ride. I was thoroughly enjoying myself until he mentioned that we had to switch positions so I could feel his whole penis. Not once, not twice, but three times. He wouldn't shut up about it. I was so annoyed. A penis didn't magically get bigger in a different position...or so I thought. When I turned around to reverse cowgirl, I was shocked to feel his nice thick joystick thrust even deeper. I was glad he couldn't see my confused and aroused expression as he guided my hips from behind. Being with him filled the emptiness inside literally and figuratively.

He knew that I could only orgasm when someone ate me out, so once he finished he laid me on the back seat and fulfilled me with some tongue acrobatics. It was exactly what I needed.

Our friends-with-benefits adventure continued for years. No strings. No jealousy. Just a couple of friends who really enjoyed each other's private parts. We still have a special friendship to this day. A timeless one that's much deeper than an orgasm.

Surround yourself with people who bring out the magic in you, not the madness.

Lord Farquaad

I crossed paths with Lord Farquaad during my stint at a clothing store, a job about as thrilling as watching paint dry on a rainy day. I couldn't count the things I'd have preferred doing to folding clothes for eight straight hours. But my very close-to-zero bank account and student loans accumulated toward a degree I would never use left me with no other choice.

Everyone has a "type" they're most attracted to. At this point in my life, my type was all over the place, but it definitely didn't include guys who stood at eye level with my five-two self. Though decent-looking, the idea of sleeping with him never crossed my mind—he was just a friendly person to chat with while we endured our boring job. When he suggested a movie night at his place, I honestly thought we were going to watch one.

We sat in his living room with nothing but the television on. As the cold winter wind howled outside, he pulled me close. I wasn't expecting to cuddle with someone, but in the ambiance of the situation, the close contact felt nice, so I settled in comfortably.

A mere thirty seconds into the movie, he casually asked if I'd like a massage. While very content where I was, I was never one to turn down a rub. He clumsily moved behind me and began kneading my shoulders. After his hands prodded me for twenty seconds without any pressure or intent, he declared it was my turn. What the hell? I didn't come over to play massage tag! Reluctantly, I switched positions with him as the realization hit me: "movie" was code for "hookup." I felt so stupid for not knowing this obvious euphemism. Before the ten-second mark ticked by, he turned around and kissed me.

It was terrible. His tongue flailed side to side like a thirsty dog that didn't know how to drink water. Was this going to be the recurring theme for all my random hookups—bad kissers? I certainly hoped not.

I was relieved when he asked for a condom. Anything was better than making out with him. Plus, I figured we had already reached the peak of awkwardness. Things couldn't possibly get any worse.

I was wrong. He kept up with the canine theme by mounting and humping me like a tiny dog humps a stranger's leg. Finishing before I could blink five times. It was so awful.

I convinced myself to give him another shot by considering that he just needed a warm-up after not having intimacy in a while. Now that he got me in the mood for some dick, this couldn't be the end, right? I cradled his head and gently asked whether he was ready for round two. He coldly replied that he was too tired from his long day.

His words sent me reeling. It took every ounce of self-control to keep myself from smashing the side table lamp over his head. I literally came over to have a chill movie night, and there I sat stupidly after being used by Lord-freaking-Farquaad.

I bolted out of his place only to find a parking ticket on my windshield. Such a shit night.

Despite everything, I accepted an invitation to join him and his friends at a club the following week. Still grappling with the painful aftermath of my first breakup, I was scraping the bottom of the social barrel for company. When Lord Farquaad and I had a minute alone together, he audaciously planted his tiny hand on my thigh and, in a high-pitched, whiney tone, declared that he was "horny." I cringed as I used my thumb and forefinger to grab his wrist and drop it back onto his own lap. If my actions didn't give him the hint, my repulsed expression surely did. I was offended that he actually believed there was a snowball's chance in a microwave of his little pee-pee getting anywhere near me again. Fuck that.

Your body is not a destination of convenience for those who offer nothing in exchange for their presence.

Lip Lad

It was six months post-break-up. I found myself on a self-destructive path as a way to cope. My life revolved around sex, drugs, and alcohol, with the sole purpose of numbness and revenge. My ex had escalated his harassment to a new level of vile, moving beyond voicemails and texts to publicly shaming me. He exposed all our intimate moments and conversations to everyone I knew, distorting them to portray me as a monster. What made it worse was that he lived along the main road I had to take to school every day. Each time he spotted me he would unleash a torrent of obscenities for the whole neighborhood to hear. Whore, slut, dirty bitch, and stupid cunt were his favorites.

I knew his words weren't true, but it still stung that someone I secretly cared about could say such horrible things to me. I had to make him hurt back. I knew my promiscuity ate him from the inside so I decided to wield it as my weapon. Making him jealous would inflict more damage than any words.

I had always viewed Lip Lad as just a friend until I remembered my ex's distaste for him. This memory promoted him to the VIP section of my "To Sleep With" list.

It was at this point in my life that I realized the power I held as a woman. Whenever I expressed my sexual intentions, I almost always ended up getting laid. This was liberating; I was done with subtleties and dancing around the obvious. If I desired someone or something, they would know it, and I would have it.

Lip Lad and I scheduled a rendezvous immediately following a brief and straight-to-the-point phone powwow.

After enduring a thirty-minute bus ride to his place, he informed me that he didn't have any condoms. I was irritated at myself for forgetting to bring them and at him for not considering the necessity. I had literally delivered myself to him with enough notice to get prepared for the occasion. Having condoms on hand was the least he could have done. The public transportation experience had already put me off, and now I was thoroughly unimpressed. It took another hour to walk to the store and back to his place.

I was very over it as we stepped into his room, but I took a deep breath and pushed forward with the reason I had come. He lay on his bed and pulled me on top of him so that we could make out, but his huge lips remained motionless. I enthusiastically tried to initiate some reciprocation by moving from his lips to his cheek, neck, and then back up to where I'd started, but he proceeded to act like a fucking statue. I paused to see whether he was being playful, but nothing changed when I resumed. So there I was, licking the face of a sculpture. Did he think this was hot? What could possibly be running through his mind to make him believe that this was okay? Was this a foreshadow of what was to come? I was as turned off as a light switch during a power outage.

At this point my whole body was screaming no. The sole anchor that held me there was the anticipation of the hurt my ex would experience upon learning that I'd let Lip Lad inside of me. But was revenge worth doing something I didn't want to do? My body continued to scream no as I clumsily took off my pants. It screamed no even louder as he approached me with the condom in place. I wasn't very good at hiding emotions so I could only imagine the contorted expression he saw as he positioned himself on top of me. My mind kept making excuses to stay.

My ex would hate this.
I can't just leave. Lip Lad is a friend.
My ex would hate this.
I've already come this far—
might as well finish what I started.
My ex would hate this.

I was frozen on his bed as he held his penis in his hand, ready to enter me. I was disgusted. With him and myself. While he wasn't unappealing, I had no sexual feelings toward him. Witnessing him naked further confirmed my lack of attraction. He thrust himself inside of me with the same stoicism he used when kissing. Barely moving in and out as I lay there praying for him to be done. I never wanted something to end so badly. After what seemed an eternity, he informed me that he was ready to come. I heaved a sigh of relief as the glow at the end of the tunnel emerged. To my dismay, he pulled out and started to remove the condom. He was about to shoot his load on top of me, which was a definite "Hell-fucking-no." I have never hell-no'd more in my life. That was the last straw. Nope, nope, nope! I told him to finish himself off in the bathroom as I hightailed out of there as fast as I could. Just *no*.

Did I immediately text a shady "friend" about what I'd done because I knew they would run and tell my ex? Yes. Was it worth it? Not in the grand scheme of things. I ruined a good friendship and took away from the very essence of myself—my integrity and my sense of self-respect.

Cutting off your nose to spite your face has a price that only you will pay.

Spiky-Hair Dude

I was anything but okay. It had been seven months since my breakup, and my thoughts were still tangled up with my ex. The only solace I could find was at the bottom of a cheap bottle while lost in the rhythm of the dance floor. That was where I encountered Spiky-Hair Dude—someone I recognized from my first high school but had never really talked to. I remember my friends swooning over him, but I hadn't shared their sentiment—his hair reminded me of Sonic the Hedgehog. Yet in that hazy moment, I knew he'd be the perfect distraction from the shadows in my soul.

I staggered over to him in my intoxicated state, initiating a conversation that quickly escalated into a passionate kissing session with the whole club as our audience. I didn't care. We swapped numbers and sexted until I was at his house the following night.

Contrary to my belief that all guys were sex-hungry assholes, he turned out to be a genuine sweetheart. We spent hours on his bed, engaged in deep conversations as the sun slowly made its way through the curtains. When he finally leaned in for a kiss, it was soft and tender. He took his time tracing the contours of my body with his lips, showing an appreciation for me that I hadn't felt for myself in a long while. This was nice. Our connection felt even stronger when he placed himself inside of me sensually and rocked to the rhythm my body asked for. I had closed my eyes to relish the beautiful moment we were having when he abruptly stopped, whispering that his mother was in the kitchen just outside his room.

Great. I had a blast chatting all night, but did he not consider the time constraint before waiting an eternity to make his move? I had zero intention of meeting the parents. The only escape route was the front door, in plain sight from the kitchen. Fantastic. He decided that the best plan would be for me to hide in his closet until he could sneak me out when he left for school. So there I sat, perched on a box behind his clothes, eavesdropping on a morning conversation between a guy I'd known for a whopping twenty-four hours and his mom. I laughed to myself at the predicament I was in. All I'd wanted was a little no-strings-attached dick, and there I was, the hidden guest of honor in a closet. Guess today was not the day. He went about his morning routine as I tried not to make any suspicious noises. You know, like breathing.

As soon as he was audibly in the shower, his mother walked into his room. She stood there for a solid five minutes, scrutinizing the scene before her. She knew something was up. Mom senses are no joke. I held my breath, resisting the urge to jump out and give her the scare of a lifetime. If I was going to get caught, might as well make it memorable. I began pulsing with adrenaline as she slowly approached the closet. Thankfully, the sound of the shower shutting off snapped her out of detective mode, and she quickly left the room. Close call.

As Spikey-Hair Dude distracted her, I bolted out of his room, out the front door, and down the street faster than a caffeinated cheetah. I could've run the ten miles home with all the adrenaline pumping through me. Mission successful.

Although the sex part lasted about five seconds, we had been intimate with each other in a different way. He would never know it, but he respected me at a point in my life where I didn't respect myself. We never saw each other again, but I always remembered him—and that closet.

> *A good man will remind you of the beauty you carry within yourself.*

Wannabe Gangster

I encountered Wannabe Gangster through an unfortunate association with Becky (let's call her that), my ex's loser cousin. At twenty-six, she was unemployed and proved to be neither a good friend nor person to my nineteen-year-old self. She was, in fact, a dirty, sneaky bitch. The only reason I maintained any association with her was because she could buy me alcohol and provide my ex a play-by-play on everything I did after I drank it. And let me tell you, I gave her a show.

Night after night, we met up to party—clubs, bars, parks, houses—anywhere we could get our hands on things to get us fucked up. I danced and flirted with anyone who gave me the slightest attention. Hiding my tormented soul under a mask of intoxicated happiness. My ex needed to believe I was living my best life for me to be able to fuel his obvious jealousy. I relished the idea that I could still get under his skin while feigning indifference to the hurtful shade he threw at me. I hated that I still craved his attention, but in my twisted mind, it affirmed he still cared for me. Even deeper than that, I held onto the hope that if he would just apologize for what he'd done, we could be together again. I didn't know whether I'd ever be able to move on from him. I wondered whether everyone's first breakup was this toxic.

It was a Tuesday night at Becky's apartment. Two unfamiliar boys had followed her into her room. My focus was solely on the bottle of vodka in my hands, so I initially brushed off her shouting for me to join. After she screeched my name for the fifth time, I reluctantly went to see what she could possibly want. I walked in to find the three of them crammed onto the bed—Becky was tangled up with the scrawny guy, and it was clear the other was meant for me. I lay down beside him briefly, but as soon as he leaned in to kiss me, I bolted. No amount of drunkenness could convince me to join this chaotic love circus with a girl I hated and guys whose names were still a mystery to me.

My designated guy followed me as I stepped outside for a smoke. Before I could light it up, he cradled my face like it was the last piece of pizza at a party and declared that I was the most beautiful girl he had ever seen and no one compared to how amazing I was…blah, blah, blah. I rolled my eyes as I proceeded with my nicotine fix. He'd known me for one minute.

He continued serenading me with pleasantries as I finished my smoke. Although fully aware it was verbal diarrhea, I felt an odd satisfaction at having nice words directed at me. Most terms that echoed in my mind involved the remnants of my ex's nasty voicemails. So I let Shakespeare-on-crack perform for another twenty minutes before chugging the rest of the vodka and leading him to the back seat of my car. I was bored and hadn't had sex in over a month. This had the potential to be fun. As a bonus, I knew Becky would make sure my deeds would be publicized as needed.

As soon as my underwear came off, Wannabe Ganster's tune changed. He began demanding I contort into all these uncomfortable positions as I bounced on his huge penis. All while he sat there lifelessly. Talk about wasted gifts. As soon as he finished he asked me (verbatim): "Did you think my sex game was terrible?" I spit a little as I laughed in his face, confirming the assumptions he had about himself. He was very upset as he proclaimed, "You're not my girlfriend so I don't need to fuck you right." Barf.

I quickly discovered that he had a pregnant girlfriend and was actively looking for a "side bitch." Wannabe Gangster blatantly laid out his scheme, fully expecting me to be on board with it. He was a joke, just like his useless penis. The realization that I had spared him a single second of my time made me nauseous. I didn't care how much I wanted sex or how low I was in my life. I refused to provide this scummy loser with more of my time. Hard pass.

Boys will treat you according to the standards you set and the behavior you accept.

Final Revenge Boy

I was at the peak of my vindictive hurricane of existence. Rock bottom had a basement—that was my residence, and I would do anything to ensure that my ex shared the space with me.

Deep down I didn't want this. I was so tired of the pain. I wanted peace and love. I hated the thought of my ex with other people. I longed for him to be exclusively mine again. Alcohol no longer numbed, so I clung to the idea that enduring these storms would eventually lead us back together. Proving to the world that we could make it through adversity as a united force.

I wish I'd had someone wiser than me back then to slap me into reality.

The day I decided to tell him I was done competing in the pain olympics was the same day I realized we had zero chance of getting back together. I arranged a meet-up with the intention of having an honest, mature conversation free of arguments. He agreed, but when I arrived, he pulled a sneak attack—while his friend distracted me, he swiped

$500 worth of marijuana stashed in my car. I was livid. It was the final straw. I didn't feel hurt anymore. In its place was pure rage. There was no turning back.

I strategically became closer to all his friends, ensuring their loyalty was to me. Not a hard strategy to pull off, considering I was their drug dealer. They quickly evicted him from their shared apartment to prioritize my presence over his. There was nothing stopping me now. When all his belongings were packed up and thrown on the porch for pick-up, my new posse made sure to give me a heads-up. I raced over and took everything, leaving my ex with nothing to his name.

I reveled in satisfaction as his harassing phone calls and voicemails ramped up. I knew I had hit the nerve I was aiming for. I had endured his antics for so long that nothing he said fazed me anymore, especially as the fire from his burning belongings warmed me under the starry night. The feeling was glorious.

I won. I knew it. He knew it. Yet my ex decided to take it to another level. Idiot.

He attempted to taunt me with messages insinuating that he was screwing one of my closest friends. This dumbass clearly hadn't learned the consequences of fucking with me. I had nothing to lose—and had no close friends.

The next day I led his best friend into an empty room at a party and slowly crawled on top of him until I reached his lips. My body quivered at the sweet taste of vengeance. He was as hungry for me as I for him. My pants were ripped off ravenously before he dived under my underwear head first. It would've felt good if he hadn't maneuvered my legs over my head to fold me in half at my neck. I wondered what porno he'd seen this level of contortion on. I was five seconds away from tapping out when he pulled a condom out of his pocket to really get the party started. Thank God.

After being inside me for about five minutes, he exclaimed that he "couldn't do it," loud enough for the people outside to hear. He couldn't keep it up. I didn't care. The deed was done.

You could have offered me a fortune to wipe the smile off my face, and it still wouldn't have budged. Especially while I watched someone at the party text the news to my ex. This was my final parting gift and the best/worst sex of my life!

I blocked him on everything before he could resume blowing up my phone. It was well past time to move forward. My ex got everything he deserved. Plus, revenge was exhausting. I finally realized that he had never been the person for me. The only thing we had in common was our mutual physical attraction to each other. He was nothing but a deadweight loser with no place in my life.

Trying to destroy someone's life is the quickest way to destroy your own. The best revenge is happiness.

My Fingers

The view was glorious as I rose from rock bottom. Free from the baggage of toxic people and situations, I was starting anew, ready to embrace the world with a fresh mind and heart. To celebrate my fresh start, I decided to learn how to make myself come. It would be my first step in getting reacquainted with myself after the long hiatus.

I took off all my clothes and lay on my bed with my head propped up by a pillow. I placed two fingers on my clit and rubbed from side to side. I changed the motion to a slow circle but was still getting nowhere. I could sense the heat building, but it was still far from that tingling feeling I would get right before an orgasm. I wondered what someone would think if they were watching me. What did my face look like? I moved one of my fingers in and slowly out again as I returned my mind back to myself. I liked this, so I added more fingers and experimented with different movements to see what turned me on most. Feeling the tightness of my pussy press against my fingers aroused me, even more so when I used the tips to make a summoning motion. So I continued fingering myself. I used my other hand to squeeze my nipples and brush around my thighs for different sensations. After an hour and a lot of vigorous finger action, I almost gave up. Why wasn't it working?

I remembered that penetration alone never finished me off so I took out my two fingers and placed them back on my clit. I welcomed the feeling of cool wetness from my aroused lady parts. This felt much better than when I'd started. I circled around as I began to feel a buildup. I alternated between inserting my fingers and rubbing my clit until I knew to focus on the outside. I stopped the circling and moved my fingers forcefully back and forth until I could feel a burn in my arm accompanied by that familiar pre-orgasm tingle. I was close. My arm was tired, but I was committed. My breath became shallow as my insides started to race. Faster and faster until the intense sensation of pleasure exploded down my spine. I lay there in a glow of self-love as my whole body reveled in the aftermath.

I had done it. It took about two hours of sheer determination, but it was well worth it.

I would never have orgasm-less sex again. Or sex at all for that matter. Unless I wanted it.

Mr. BBQ

I met Mr. BBQ at a barbecue in June. Before we even spoke, he gave me a lingering look that clearly said, "I want to be naked with you." We exchanged numbers as soon as we had a moment alone.

He embodied perfection—an urban man with a sophisticated style and an unwavering interest in me. Over the next few weeks, he invited me everywhere: clubs, parks, houses…you name it. He showered me with flowers, drinks, and cocaine as we danced the nights away. In his presence, I felt not just beautiful but also deeply desired—a vital salve for my soul as I continued along the path of rebuilding myself.

It was late on a weeknight when we arrived at his friend's place, the air buzzing with lively conversations as people indulged in the mountain of cocaine on the coffee table. Mr. BBQ and I were eager to catch up. With a confident flair, he expertly prepared a line for me while proudly introducing me to everyone I hadn't yet met. Watching his genuine enthusiasm for my presence made my insides melt.

He stayed by my side all evening, continually expressing his affection through tender touches and warm glances. We mingled for as long as we could, but eventually, our desires became irresistible. After sharing one last monster line, we quietly slipped away to the privacy of my car.

We passionately kissed as I straddled him in the front seat. I loved it when no space was between us. He grabbed my butt from under my dress and pulled me closer as the intensity of our make-out session increased. Feeling him harden made me want him even more. There was only one issue. We didn't have a condom. I was slightly disappointed but also a little glad. As much as I wanted him right then and there, I didn't want our first time to be squished in a car. I informed him about my firm "no glove, no love" policy, and he reassured me not to worry.

I was relieved to be with someone so understanding. Our make-out session persisted as he gently removed my thong. While I suspected he wanted to explore with his fingers, I reminded him once more about my insistence on protection. He reassured me he understood as he unveiled his penis. I wasn't worried. I trusted him. I was so horny that I figured we could dry-hump without penetration, right?

Five minutes later I realized his penis had been inside of me the whole time. I had mistaken it for his fingers because it was so minuscule. I was bewildered. All of this had unfolded while he'd calmly repeated his reassuring mantra of "Don't worry" in a soothing tone. He was doing what I specifically told him I didn't want while comforting me? That was fucked.

I calmly hopped off his millimeter-peter and informed him that I had to go. He whined and begged me to stay. Fuck that and hell, no. Absolutely not. How dare he blatantly disrespect me like that? I hugged him goodbye as if I would definitely see him again and left without looking back. He called and texted me every day afterward but would never get another chance with me. What he'd done had been rapey.

Those who fail to respect your body and words deserve no place in your life. Feel your power as you walk away from things that do not honor you as a woman!

GBF

Ever have a condom fall out of you a week after sex? I wish I could say I hadn't. How it had stayed inside me for so long was beyond my comprehension. I swear I shower.

It all began at my new job at a banquet hall conveniently located near my college and far removed from the scummy people I had been entangled with for the past two years. At twenty, I was eager for a fresh start. After struggling through my first semesters, plagued by poor mental health, partying, and indecision, I finally committed to a bachelor's degree in health science. Though challenging, I felt a surge of excitement from my newfound passion for learning and the opportunities it would bring.

New atmosphere, new friends, new job, new life. I was living again.

On my first day, GBF trained me. Though I felt like a lost puppy trailing him throughout the shift, I found myself enjoying his company. He was charismatic, tall, and handsome, with a shared love for partying. In fact, the entire wait staff seemed to embrace that same spirit. I was welcomed into the group right away, and for the first time in a long time, I felt like I truly belonged.

After every shift, we made a ritual of grabbing a bottle of Grey Goose on our way to GBF's house. Night after night, we danced on the counters and sang at the top of our lungs. There was no drama, no heartache—just carefree, drunken fun. I had never partied this much in my entire life. These were the friends I had been yearning for, and I was genuinely happy.

After going particularly hard one evening, I made the responsible choice not to drive home drunk. Another guy had the same thought, which led to an unexpected situation: all three of us squeezed into GBF's bed, with him in the middle. I thought it was a little gay but chalked it up to the alcohol and settled in to sleep.

I was about to start my first dream when I felt GBF kissing my shoulder. I had no intention of fucking anyone that night, but the sex goddess within hadn't been out to play in a couple of months, so she was easily convinced. I turned around and kissed him back.

In an instant, I found myself lifted into the air and tossed onto the dresser in a dramatic outburst of passion. The commotion caused by everything tumbling off the cluttered surface inevitably roused the random guy on the other side of the bed. I was not about to give him a show, so I made GBF carry me to the bathroom to finish what we started. He bent me over the bathtub and gave it to me slow and deep while I tested out my newly acquired self-stimulation abilities. Boy, did they work! We climaxed together loudly. I was thoroughly satisfied.

Any lingering positive feelings from the night before evaporated the moment I walked into work the next day. It was clear that everyone knew what had happened. I was so embarrassed. As I passed the kitchen, staff members whispered about me in their language while casting smirks and disapproving glances my way. I couldn't grasp their judgment; we were all adults. I had simply slept with someone I liked. I felt foolish and ashamed and never wanted to show my face again. My hopes for a fresh start had been crushed.

For the next week, shame weighed heavily on me until I had an epiphany: The chatter around me wasn't mockery; it was admiration. I had unwittingly gained a fan club. Armed with this newfound perspective, I carried myself with extra confidence for the next month until the tabloids got ahold of a new headline story. Nothing would be allowed to derail my new beginning. I did what I did and would never be ashamed of it.

A month after the fiasco and three weeks after the condom fell out of me, GBF came out as well. Everyone saw that coming but me. But what would life be without surprises?

We ended up working together for eight years of absolute hilarity. He's still my Gay Best Friend to this day. I am so grateful I didn't quit.

The whispers of others only hold power if you allow them to.

Pedro

Oh, Pedro. Such a genuinely lovely human—to me, that is. Not sure how he treated his girlfriend of seven years who was left in the dust as soon as we met. I'll elaborate.

Our paths crossed while working at a summer camp together. It was my sixth year, and his first. Despite not being my usual type—with his blond hair and blue eyes—I found myself undeniably attracted to him. Our first interaction happened during a supposedly "friendly" staff bonding soccer game. While I was focused on securing a victory, his attention was directed toward me. Completely oblivious, I elbowed (him) and kicked my way to a win. No time for crushes when you're crushing. I was still sweaty and riding the high of my victory when he asked for my number. Flattered, I told him how honored I felt that he wanted to add a winner to his contact list. I laughed while everyone looked at me like I was weird. Good thing I never relied on others to recognize my sense of humor.

The next day, he invited me to join him for beer and wings. After barely surviving eight hours with one hundred screaming kids on a Wednesday, I settled onto my couch, ready to type out a firm *Hell, no*. But just as I was about to hit send, a lively song came on the radio resurrecting me and launching an impromptu dance party around my house. I realized that I did indeed have it in me to go out. Twenty minutes later, he picked me up.

We headed to a nearby bar, and the drinking festivities kicked off. It was then that he dropped a bombshell: His name wasn't actually Pedro—it had all been a joke. I had been calling him that for the past twenty-four hours! We shared a good laugh over it. The night rolled on casually until the female bartender randomly asked us whether we had kissed yet. I hadn't even considered it as I wiped wing sauce off my dirty face. She definitely prophesized what was to come.

During our fourth round of drinks I caught his eye while lifting the pint glass to my lips. I swam in the blueness of his irises long enough to decide that I wanted to sit on his lap naked. As soon as I set my drink down he ever so smoothly swooped in to kiss me. I was so surprised by his boldness that it took me a moment to match the rhythm of his lips. But once I did, it was perfect.

I didn't want the night to end, so upon leaving the bar, I playfully suggested that we go streaking before heading home. It was partly a whimsical idea to test his spontaneity but more so a desire to extend our time together. I sensed something incredibly special brewing between us.

We drove to a secluded parking lot, where I ripped off my clothes and sprinted off. He did the same, effortlessly catching up to me. I was mesmerized by his beautifully sculpted athletic physique.

It had been such an unexpectedly wonderful night—until he dropped me off at home. As we shared a goodbye kiss, I jokingly remarked that I hoped he didn't have a girlfriend. The slight hesitation of his lips stopped my breathing. This jerk wasn't fucking single! After everything?! I was pissed. In a fit of frustration, I declared that it would never work between us and slammed the door behind me as I stormed off.

I couldn't believe it. Had he no shame for leading me on like that? I thought we shared a genuine connection. Lost in my thoughts, I eventually arrived at a self-centered conclusion: How he chose to navigate his life was none of my concern. My sexual desires took precedence over his obvious failed relationship. It was evident that he didn't care much about his partner if he could cheat so effortlessly. I wanted to sleep with him and that was that. I would use him for his penis and then bid farewell at the end of the summer. He could go deal with his issues after our fling had run its course.

A couple of days later, after a regrettable episode of cocaine in a dingy club bathroom, I concluded that I'd prefer having sex than partaking in a drug-fueled escapade with my hot-mess girlfriends. I had moved past that phase in my life while they were still roaring through theirs. Having communicated my changed perspective to Pedro regarding our situation the day before, he, true to form, was there to pick me up within ten minutes of my call.

He didn't recognize me at first as I approached his car. My hair was straightened to perfection, and my tight mini dress accentuated all my womanly curves. I looked a far cry from my usual homeless camp counselor vibe. It wasn't until I opened the passenger door that realization hit him. The look on his face was priceless—eyebrows raised in delightful surprise at how well I cleaned up.

We went straight to his bedroom, where I fit perfectly in his arms. As the effects of the drugs began to fade, I found myself embracing a different kind of high. We passionately kissed while we pressed our bodies together. It felt so right! As I was on my back, he got off the bed and told me to hold the pillow behind my head. He grabbed my legs and pulled me effortlessly to the edge. He got on his knees and placed my feet on his shoulders as I watched with my head supported. I loved being manhandled. He gave me his tongue like it was his last meal on earth. I came twice.

He then scooped me up with his strong arms and placed my back against the wall beside the bed. He entered me for the first time with my arms around his neck and his hands firmly holding me by my thighs. He bounced me up and down his perfectly sized cock and then demanded that I watch him fuck me in the mirror behind him. I submitted to him as I relished his masculinity. I was so turned on. Watching his muscular ass flex every time he thrust into me was something I never knew I needed to see. It was so hot. Our sexual chemistry was through the roof. He threw me back onto the bed, where we climaxed in sync as the world and all its issues faded into nothing. This was better than any of those empty sexcapades I'd had out of anger and revenge. This was what being intimate with someone was supposed to feel like!

At the end of summer, he ended his relationship with his girlfriend, and we embarked on a beautiful two-year journey together. During that time, he surrounded me with the kind of love and unwavering affection that every woman deserves. I felt genuinely cherished every single moment. Despite his limited finances, he always found ways to surprise me with thoughtful gifts and romantic gestures. He was attentive, kind, and steadfast in his support, making me feel like a priority above all else. He would have given me the world if he could. Regrettably, I knew he wasn't the one for me.

He seemed perfect in every way, but when I looked into his eyes, I didn't feel the deep connection you should when you know you want to wake up with that person every day for the rest of your life. I tried to love him as deeply as he did me, but it just wasn't there, and I found myself longing to be with other men. It was a heart-wrenching decision, but ultimately, I had to say goodbye.

Although difficult, goodbyes are necessary. Just because someone is a good person does not mean they are the right one for you.

Parking Prince

I broke up with Pedro because I wanted to sit on Parking Prince's dick. While not the sole reason, it was certainly something to look forward to ease the guilt of shattering a good man's heart.

Parking Prince was a valet at the banquet hall where I worked—muscular, handsome, and fresh out of high school. He was eighteen, and I was about to graduate college at age twenty-three. He was still a toddler in the life/women experience category, so I ignored his attempts to park his charm on me for a solid five months. Plus, I had a boyfriend.

Parking Prince always seemed to appear wherever I was—be it the kitchen, dining room, or smoking section. Out of nowhere, I'd be swept off my feet by a surprise bear hug from behind. Despite reminding him that his age wasn't my thing, and oh yeah, I wasn't single, his constant pursuit made me start to catch feelings for him. He refused to let any factor hold him back from pursuing me. His boldness made my pussy so wet.

Parking Prince was the first person I told about my change in relationship status. We were sharing a smoke during one of our breaks when I casually mentioned it. He looked at me in disbelief, then leaned in to kiss me after I confirmed it. Every fiber of my being had craved that moment. His touch and the taste of his lips sent me soaring, but what really captivated me was his unique scent. It wasn't the usual cologne; instead, it was a subtle mix of sweat and the spearmint gum he was chewing. It was something new for me—I had never felt so drawn to someone's pheromones before.

After a week of sneaking around and making out all over our workplace, I started to sense that something was off. He wasn't popping up around every corner like he used to, and our interactions became less frequent. It felt like he was backing off from his previous full-on pursuit of almost six months. I was so confused—now that we could finally enjoy each other, it seemed like he wasn't as interested anymore. What the fuck?

So I turned to drinking—every day, before, during, and after work—trying to wrap my head around the situation. I was dripping in desire for him and couldn't handle the fact that he no longer reciprocated. The worst part was the constant phone checks, hoping each notification was from him. I kept ruminating over our interactions and messages, searching for clues as to what I could've said to make him lose interest.

I finally hit the "fuck it" point at midnight after a long day at work and a few hours at the bar. I sent him a casual *are you up?* text, thinking if I got ignored, I could just blame the alcohol. To my surprise, he invited me over. I was ecstatic—maybe there was still a chance to rekindle what we had.

I wasn't exactly prepared for the occasion since I ran to the bar right after work. Luckily, my gay best friend lived nearby, so I made a quick pit stop for a shower and some last-minute grooming with my trusty glove compartment emergency shaver. By the time I was ready, it was already 2 a.m. I had no choice—I couldn't let my vagina make an entrance like a Christmas wreath!

He led me to his room as soon as I arrived. I had sobered up enough to sense his diminished interest, and it stung. I wanted him to want me again. I tried to charm him back with the humor he used to laugh at, but all I got was a bored expression. To make matters worse, his responses made me feel like I couldn't tell a good story to save my life. It felt like I was clinging to a sinking ship.

I guess this was my karma for breaking Pedro's heart. Whatever. I might as well get an orgasm out of this.

His skin was soft like his forced-passionate, uncaring kisses. I took my time down his body as I breathed in the scent that I'd craved since the first time our lips met. Back when he was interested in me, he'd mentioned how much he loved blowjobs so I wanted to give him one he would never forget.

I French-kissed the tip of his dick with my tongue before using it to trace down and back up his shaft. I did that a couple of times before stopping at the underside of the head. I knew this was one of the most sensitive places for guys, so I gently kissed it before licking it slowly with the tip of my tongue. I could feel that he liked that, so I stayed there in a steady rhythm. Connecting more of my tongue with each lap. It felt like he was about to come, so I left the pleasure space and tasted my way down to his balls. They were soft and clean-smelling. I decided to grab them with my hand and creep my lips to his head, where I hovered long enough for him to feel my breath. He was begging me with his hips to put it inside. I looked up at him through my eyelashes and relished in the pleasure on his face. I felt my mouth water for him as I wrapped my lips around his head and slowly took him in. He called me a "good girl" out of nowhere, and I nearly orgasmed. No one had ever called me that before, and I liked it. I started to feel him throb as I pumped up and down with my mouth, so I knew he was close to finishing. He hadn't made any effort to pleasure me, so I stopped abruptly and walked my vag up to his face. I had enough one-sided sexual experiences to know that I was not down for another one. His skilled tongue was impressive. I didn't think someone as young as him would know what to do. Before I finished I suggested that we have sex. Oral orgasms are fun, but I liked penetrative ones better.

    I climbed on top of him and bounced as hard as I could. I had so much pent-up frustrations about him that I needed to feel friction. He immediately made me stop because the headboard was banging the wall he shared with his sister. We moved to the floor but couldn't continue because he lost his erection along the way. I could tell he was embarrassed. So I tried not to show how annoyed I was at the waste of a good blowjob.

I put my shorts back on as we lay there talking about what was going on between us and why he was acting differently. This fucker told me that I had been trying too hard, which had turned him off. So when a guy tries to impress a girl for six fucking months, it's cute, but if a girl shows interest back, it's trying too hard? Fucker.

I should've just left, but I was still so horny for him that the hopes of getting the D left me rooted. When he finally got his second wind, he romantically tried to stick it in through the leg hole of my shorts. *What the actual fuck?* I had patiently waited through all this nonsense for him to wake his dick up, and he wanted to try to fuck me through my jean shorts? Hell, no. I pulled them off for easier access, and he pumped twice and shot his load. I didn't even get a moment to touch myself. All this for five unsatisfying seconds? That blowjob I gave him was some of my best work. What a waste of time! Vagina was not happy. I drove home as the sun came up feeling alone and used.

I wish I could say I moved on easily, but I couldn't get his scent and the thought of orgasming with him inside of me out of my mind. I reached out again only to be ghosted.

Fast-forward eight years, and out of the blue, he calls with a heartfelt apology, blaming his behavior on a bunch of irrelevant excuses and, of course, youth—just like I had warned him when he first started running his game on me. As if that wasn't audacious enough, he had the nerve to suggest I relocate closer to him so we could have a second shot at love. The audacity!

"The biggest coward is a man who awakens a woman's love without the intention of loving her"—a great quote from Bob Marley.

Tattoo Ninja

I met Tattoo Ninja at the banquet hall where I worked. He caught my eye while setting up to DJ the party, his muscles on display as he carried in the heavy speakers in a sleeveless shirt. He was strikingly hot and covered in tattoos. Throughout the night, we stole moments to chat whenever we could. Our connection felt almost destined as we discovered a shared love for everything from martial arts and extreme sports to working out, singing, and even musical theater. It felt like I had found my perfect match and was definitely itching for a pounding, especially after my last disappointing sexual encounter.

The next day, he picked me up for a classic movie date, which I enjoyed, but I wanted a more interactive setting to really get to know him. So, I suggested we hit up a bar right after. As the drinks flowed, I couldn't shake the feeling that something was off—not in a serial killer kind of way but in a mysterious way, as if he was hiding secrets behind his dark eyes. Assuming it was just paranoia, I brushed it off.

Hanging out with him one-on-one was a different experience from the day before. He was pretty socially awkward, and I ended up carrying most of the conversation. Despite our shared interests, I grew bored. Luckily, my gay friends came to the rescue with a text inviting me to join them at a club for some Pride festivities. I was totally down for that! I extended the invite to Tattoo Ninja, and to my surprise, he agreed. A guy who was confident enough to venture to a gay club with strangers was definitely someone I wanted to keep around. I shelfed his awkwardness and ordered us two shots for the road. This was going to be a great night!

We found my gays in the middle of the crowded dance floor, and our introductions had to be shouted over the blaring music. It seemed like Tattoo Ninja might have run into one of them before, but we were all too intoxicated to piece it together at that moment. It was officially party time!

Saying we had fun would be an understatement. We had the time of our lives in that club—dancing, drinking, and laughing the night away. Tattoo Ninja really came alive, and I was totally into him. I noticed his gaze lingering on the drag queens and suspected it might be his first time witnessing their fabulousness. It filled me with joy to find someone so wonderfully accepting. How had I gotten so lucky? We wrapped up the night with a big kiss when he dropped me off at home. I was looking forward to seeing him again.

The next day, the gays and I squeezed all five of us into my compact car for a lunch adventure. As we cautiously considered the possibility that they might know

Tattoo Ninja, I pulled up his Facebook on my phone, and chaos erupted. One friend, who had missed the previous night's fun, recognized him immediately and launched into a full-blown panic attack, infecting everyone in the cramped vehicle with anxiety. All he could muster was "Oh, my God…Oh, my God…I don't want to say," on repeat. This went on for so long that what was supposed to be a quick five-minute drive to the restaurant turned into a twenty-minute odyssey as I missed every possible turn. My heart was pounding like a percussion ensemble—what was the damn deal?

I finally slammed to a halt on the side of the road and demanded he spill the tea. It turned out my friends had run into Tattoo Ninja at their drag queen friend's house when they showed up unannounced. They walked in just as he was coming out of the bathroom, proudly flaunting his, ahem, monster cock. I was shook. After a quick call to their queen friend for more details, we learned that he was quite well-known in the drag community for his fetish of getting fucked by them.

I was seriously bummed. The excessive staring from the night before made sense. Now, I'd never taken issue with anyone's sexual preference, but I couldn't be with someone who fancied something I didn't have—like, you know, a penis. I genuinely thought he was into me as much as I was him. Feeling a bit lost, I decided to invite him to lunch. I figured I might as well wrangle a comedy out of this to help me forget my disappointment.

We rolled up to the restaurant before him, still in the aftermath of shock. I told the host we needed a table for five—and extra space for the elephant in the room. We almost passed out from laughter.

I downed a few tequila shots to calm my nerves before Tattoo Ninja arrived. I had to brace myself for the conversation ahead. When I met him outside, he confidently confirmed everything I had uncovered. Strangely enough, I still felt intrigued and, dare I say, wanted to experience his huge penis. Honesty and confidence always turned me on.

After a semi-awkward lunch and plenty of tequila, we headed back to my friend's place to keep the drinks flowing. Tattoo Ninja seemed more interested in entertaining the gays than giving me the attention I craved. I realized that if I wanted to take things further, I needed to isolate him from anyone sporting a dick. So, I suggested we move to my house, and he agreed. I never thought I'd find myself in a position where I had to compete with a guy for a guy!

We unwound under the stars in my backyard, with more tequila from my own stash. It was a relief to finally have his undivided attention.

I'd never been with a "gay-ish" guy before and wasn't sure what to expect when it came to his skills as a lover. While I didn't think he'd be bad, I definitely didn't foresee him being as good as he turned out to be.

He held my face firmly with both his hands as he kissed me deeply. He tasted like a yummy tequila sunrise.

I hoped I tasted the same after eight hours of drinking. I led him to my bedroom, where we slowly undressed each other. He caressed my neck with his lips while massaging my clit with his well-versed fingers, maintaining those hand motions as he used his lips to journey down. Stopping at my nipples to trace them with his tongue and nibble gently before continuing onward. It was like he had a road map to everywhere that felt good. He wasted no time in teasing my already warmed lady parts and dived in with his expert lingual muscles. Alternating his flow until he knew I was about to come. He put the condom on and eased his thick, nine-inch penis inside of me, all while continuing to circle my happy button with his fingers. I wished more guys knew about this simple technique. Once I was comfortable with receiving his whole member he lifted both of my legs over my head and rocked my world so hard I orgasmed without even having to touch myself. I was shaking by the time he pulled out and rolled over beside me. Wow.

We continued our fling for a couple weeks until it was obvious he was bored of me. I knew it was coming. He wanted the D, and I couldn't help him in that department.

There's wisdom in accepting things that are beyond your control.

LOML

In 2014, at the age of twenty-five, I eagerly boarded a cruise ship, ready to embark on what I thought would be my dream job. Much to my dismay, the "youth" staff position I accepted turned out to involve working with two- to five-year-olds instead of teenagers. Apparently, I didn't get the memo that the term "youth" meant something different in the middle of the Caribbean. Nothing says "dream job" like sitting through scream-fests by tiny overlords with diaper disasters.

It was a nightmare. I was stranded in the middle of the ocean, singing baby songs and running to hide every time someone called for a diaper-check. My colleagues hated me, but honestly, I couldn't have cared less. They were a bunch of thunder-cunts.

Ship life is something you can't really explain to anyone who hasn't lived it. You sign up thinking you're going to be globe-trotting, only to realize that "days off" don't exist and work weeks are a minimum of fifty hours. You're groomed to love six-hour "half" days, which give you a fleeting two-hour break to explore the port—if you're lucky. The endless supply of cheap booze had a way of dulling the brutal working conditions and the reality of making less than $1,500 a month. Suffice it to say, it was the toughest job I ever had.

Despite being surrounded by haters and screaming little people, I found a way to not see it as *all* bad. I had the pleasure of connecting with some incredible people from various corners of the world (in departments different from mine, of course), the food was fantastic, and port adventures, though brief, were always fun. Nights at the crew bar ended with sing-a-thons in the smoking section, and my roommate—who started the same day I did—was absolutely hilarious and quickly became one of my closest friends.

Every couple of weeks, the company would treat the staff to themed crew parties, which always promised more excitement than the typical nights at the crew bar. My roommate's and my first taste of this festive tradition was a uniform-swap theme. We couldn't stop laughing as we swam in the oversized outfits we'd borrowed from the plumber and ship security. Both a petite five-two, we could barely move under all the extra fabric. Sipping on cheap booze as we got ready turned out to be more entertaining than the actual party. I bailed for the smoking section after just fifteen minutes. It was where the real party was at anyway.

As I strolled by a ship phone, capable of connecting to any room on board, I decided that was the perfect time to booty call the ship musician I'd kissed a few nights prior. He had been running through my mind since our encounter, and I had just the right amount of liquid courage to make a move.

When he picked up, I confidently revealed my identity and asked him what he was doing in the most seductive way I could muster. Without missing a beat, he nonchalantly responded that he was "sleeping and going back to sleep." Ouch. It wasn't even late. Sleeping before 9 p.m. was unheard of in ship life. This guy serenaded me with compliments and practically begged for sex as we'd dry-humped in his bed the other night, and now he was blatantly rejecting me. I thought there was mutual interest. *Screw that,* I thought. Goodbye forever, stupid boy. No vagina for you. I felt extremely foolish and definitely unwanted. That cigarette couldn't have come fast enough.

Thankfully the smoking section was abuzz with activity. A welcome distraction from the last thirty seconds of my life. I joined a group of familiar faces and lit up my fix, grateful for the shift in focus. But the instant I looked up, my entire world stopped.

Standing there tall and proud with his well-defined arms perfectly filling out his uniform was a guy I had never seen before. *There…he…is!* screamed my inner me to myself as my eyes met the ocean blue of his. His presence took my breath and anything bad in my mind away.

He was perfection. I couldn't contain myself as I blurted out, "HIII."

He didn't catch my greeting, so the girl beside me kindly informed him that I said hello. Instead of a warm acknowledgment, he shot me a disdainful look and promptly turned away. To my relief, the ten people surrounding us stared at him in disbelief, with one even questioning whether he was gay. I laughed it off to the best of my abilities, but boy, was I humiliated. Denied twice in a matter of five minutes was embarrassing, even if I was the sole witness. I quickly finished my nicotine stick and made a swift retreat to my cabin, vowing never to let the memories of these guys anywhere near my thoughts again. This night was dead to me.

A week later, unimpressed with the crowd at the crew bar, I opted for a solo adventure in search of more appealing company. I roamed the ship in an inebriated state until I spotted some friends at a table on the lido deck. I marched over excitedly and squeezed myself into their booth. As I settled in, I looked up, only to realize that the gorgeous jerk who had snubbed me the week prior was sitting right across from me. I had managed to block him out of my mind so effectively that I didn't even notice him under my nose until it was too late.

I immediately fired up a conversation about nothing so I could cover up the agonizing urge to be anywhere but there. However, before I could finish my sentence, he interjected, 'Hey, I don't know if you recall a couple of nights ago. You tried to say hi to me and I turned away. I wanted to apologize—I had just finished work, and I was exhausted. I didn't mean to come across as rude."

My heart skipped a beat as I breathed in his words, the unexpected sincerity catching me off guard. It required every ounce of composure within me to conjure up a spicy retort and formally introduce myself. My inner sex goddess was awakened.

We broke off from the group and talked all night. He was from Eastern Europe and this was his second year working as a dealer in the ship's casino. We parted with the promise of seeing each other at the crew party the next night. I could not wait!

The music was bumping and drinks were flowing as I strived for patience amidst the persistent advances of eager suitors. In the cruise ship world, I was still labeled "fresh meat," and these men were hungry. They came at me one after another, bombarding me with questions I had no interest in answering. In an act of defense, I resorted to moving my arms around erratically to the music, ensuring a barrier that kept anyone from getting too close. My crush couldn't arrive fast enough.

I caught sight of him watching me from afar, in his captivating stance, pretending to be unfazed by the swarm of guys vying for my attention. He and I both knew we were only here for each other, so I walked over.

We drank as I danced provocatively in front of him. My panties were practically begging to come off—I couldn't wait for a sexy night with this beautiful boy. Finally sensing the anticipation, he abruptly pulled me in and asked whether he could kiss me. I gasped out a "yes" as he leaned down. About time!

We decided to grab some beers from his room before heading to the smoking section. I followed him, already knowing there was no way I was leaving once I stepped inside.

I gently nudged him toward the bed before he could get what he came for. He willingly lay down as I climbed on top of him. Pressing my forehead against his, I relished the moment before our lips met. I wanted to savor this before things escalated.

Midway through our make-out session, he commanded me to dance for him. He could have asked me to do anything, and I would have gladly obliged.

He played some music, and I sensually crawled on top. The bottom bunk of his tiny ship cabin was snug, but the close quarters heightened our senses. I slowly rolled my hips around while taking off his shirt. I could feel him growing harder beneath me as I lay my breasts against his chiseled chest. Our connection was so intense that, by the end of the song, I was on the brink of orgasm. Sliding his pants off, I delicately lowered myself onto his impressive manhood. Our bodies moved in synchronized passion as he gripped my waist with his strong hands. It wasn't long before we finished together.

We were both sweating from head to toe as we lay

beside each other panting. The past month of tension was nonexistent. I was in love, and so was he.

We showered together and returned to the bed to recover. His roommate, done with work, lay quietly on the top bunk. I paid no mind to his presence; this was the Love of My Life (LOML), and I wasn't finished playing with him. As things heated up for the second time, we crept into the bathroom and turned on the shower to muffle any noise. It was so hard to be quiet when just looking at him made sounds of pleasure slip out of my mouth. He pinned me against the door as my body pleaded for him to be inside of me again. He lifted my leg to his shoulder and kissed me intensely as he gave it to me briskly. His roommate definitely heard everything, but we didn't care.

Oh, how I loved every minute of this boy. We spent six unforgettable months sailing the seas together, and even though my contract ended two months before his, we had plans to keep our adventure going.

I went home to figure out how we would spend the rest of our lives together. Being apart was tough, but I knew it was just a temporary setback on our journey.

During that period, I felt anxious about his faithfulness. Despite knowing he loved me, the close quarters of a cruise ship without a significant other made it easy to forget about loyalty. It didn't help that I kept having a vivid dream that one of my so-called "friends" still on the ship with him had fucked him. I decided to reach out to calm my nerves. When I inquired about his interactions with other girls, she callously responded with, "You should be having this conversation with him, not me." *This bitch*. I immediately knew that something had happened. Having his Facebook password, given to me some time ago, I delved into his inbox for answers. There it was—an incriminating message from her, asking if he had told me. I responded as him with a *yes, I had to*. She immediately messaged me an apology, claiming it was a one-time mistake that meant nothing. Fuckers! I was proud of my detective skills but still devastated at the findings. I ended the relationship with a text that simply said, *I hope it was worth it*. If someone can take a man from you, he's theirs. Done.

For several weeks, he relentlessly tried to call me from the ship, even going so far as to have mutual friends plead on his behalf for another chance. But I ignored him. There was no space for reconciliation—he had betrayed me.

For a while, I was consumed by anger, but eventually, I came to see that things had unfolded for the best. We came from entirely different worlds, and maintaining a relationship across the globe would be more challenging than fulfilling—especially for two broke cruise ship workers. In the end, I forgave him and found the strength to move on.

Even after ten years, the memory of us running through the ship together still flickers in my mind from time to time. I will never forget our love story.

The act of forgiveness is not solely for the person who wronged you; it's a transformative gift you give to yourself. Set yourself free from the confines of anger. Forgive.

The Italian

I met The Italian at a train station in Italy six years prior. My friends and I were clearly lost, struggling with a map, when he kindly offered to help. Not only was his English flawless, but he was also headed to our destination. It was nice to spend time with such a warm, genuine local.

We spent the train ride getting to know each other, and by the time we arrived at our destination, he graciously invited us to spend the weekend at his family's home in the Tuscan countryside. We were thrilled by the chance to have an authentic Italian experience.

The next day, he picked up me and my girlfriend with one of his friends and a generous stash of weed. We got high as we sped through the picturesque hills and winding country roads. Our faces ached from laughing so much.

I had no idea what to expect when he invited us to his home, but the sight that greeted us far exceeded any expectation. Beyond his security gate stood an elegant Italian villa, perched atop the driveway, with chickens darting about and dogs lounging in the shade. My friend's eyebrows kissed her hairline in astonishment. I felt the same. It was like stepping into a scene from an Oscar-winning Italian romance. We were warmly introduced to his entire extended family, all of whom embraced us with open arms.

As dinner was being prepared, The Italian led us on a tour of his sprawling estate. We wandered through perfectly manicured hedges while he plucked olives and fruits for us to taste. It was nothing short of divine. Just when we thought the day couldn't get more enchanting, he took us to a secluded spot to watch the sun set over the rolling hills. I had never seen anything like it; "perfection" seemed far too small a word to capture the magic of that moment.

We ended our visit with a feast fit for royalty and a conversation that flowed as if we were old friends. It was the kind of experience every traveler dreamed of.

I kept in touch with The Italian because he was studying an hour away from my home in America—a reminder of just how small the world can be. While we occasionally met up, I never developed any romantic or sexual feelings for him until I was freshly cheated on by the LOML.

It had been about five years since we first met, and The Italian had been steadily climbing the ranks at a prestigious financial firm. He was the company's top closer, so they flew him to different cities across the US every other week. It just so happened that his work brought him to the very city I was living in at the precise moment

I needed a distraction—regardless of whether I was interested in him. He invited me to join him for dinner at an upscale restaurant.

Over a bottle of fine wine, we reminisced about our first meeting, savoring oysters as we relived the memories. As the evening unfolded, I felt a chemistry between us that never existed before. We left the restaurant hand in hand, laughing as we skipped down the cobblestone street. We hardly noticed the cold February air. He pulled me close beneath the soft glow of the hanging lights and kissed me, erasing the heartbreak I'd carried from the week before.

I wanted him, but alas, I hadn't shaved! I never expected to feel this drawn to him, so I hadn't thought to womanscape. I was kicking myself for neglecting to even consider the possibility. As much as I wanted to accept his invitation to his hotel, I declined with the truth. Although he insisted it didn't matter, I'd have rather punched a cactus than get intimate for the first time without proper grooming. I apologized and promised I'd see him the following night instead.

The next day, we met at the lobby bar of his luxurious hotel. As we shared drinks, he leaned in to kiss me. But as his breath met mine, and I felt the rhythm of his tongue, my initial excitement shifted into unease. I had enjoyed our kiss more the day before. It became clear that my attraction to him wasn't as strong as I'd thought. So, I ordered shots until the unease subsided.

Upon reaching the room, we didn't waste any time

getting to the point. The additional drinks certainly reignited a sense of connection between us. I thoroughly enjoyed our intimate encounter; his expertise in pleasuring me both with his presence and his tongue surpassed expectations I hadn't even considered having.

We lay together after round one, continuing the dirty deed with our words. Our topic of conversation: blowjobs. I had never been a fan of giving them on the first date, but in the aftermath of my recent breakup, I found myself indifferent to most things I used to care about. This propelled us into round two.

It was hot. We took the little we knew about each other from the first round and made sure to add more of it into the second. He skillfully gave me his dick as I kneeled in front of him, hands held onto the headboard and his arms wrapped around me so that he could hold my breasts. Following my climax, he withdrew and turned me around to finish in my mouth. Fully immersed in the moment, I enveloped his tip and allowed him to release inside.

HUGE MISTAKE! I had never tasted semen so terrible in my life. I gagged and nearly threw up my whole stomach. It was the absolute worst thing that ever touched my tongue. My face scrunched up, and before I could stop myself blurted out, "Ew, did you just pee in my mouth?" That was what I would imagine pee to taste like! It was that bad.

He looked extremely embarrassed as I went to rinse my mouth out with soap. I wanted to eat the soap. I think

I swallowed a piece—on purpose. We had a five-minute chat on what determined someone's flavor before I practically flew to the door to get away.

In hindsight, I see that I didn't handle the situation very kindly. He was a friend, and as disgusted as I felt, my reaction likely left him scarred.

Everyone has their own unique scent and flavor; it's never right to embarrass someone for something that's inherent to them.

Disco Dan

A couple of weeks after the sperm-tasting fiasco, I went on a snowboard trip to Colorado with some party-loving friends. Still nursing the wounds of my recent breakup, the combination of carving down a mountain by day and indulging in drugs all night was very therapeutic.

For the first couple evenings we ripped monster lines of blow until the sun came up. By day three we knew it was time to give our noses a much-needed break, so we switched to magic mushrooms. We were wide-eyed and soaring by 5 p.m. The two-bedroom cottage descended into pandemonium as the eight of us ran around, grappling with what to do. It was absolutely fantastic.

Once we descended from our psychedelic high to a somewhat normal level, one brave soul suggested heading to a club. Though a bit worn out from the festivities, I was never one to be the party pooper. We rallied the rest of the group and made our way to the village in the frigid cold.

The moment we stepped inside, we froze in unison, mesmerized by the lights dancing around us. We burst into laughter, realizing just how far from sober we really were.

While waiting in line for coat check, a tall blond guy approached me. His style struck a perfect balance between casual and put-together, signaling he wasn't the broke ski bum-type like me and my friends. Though not exactly my usual dark-haired preference, his offer to buy me a drink was all I needed to follow him to the bar—especially given my empty wallet. After some small talk, we decided to hit the dance floor. Just as I readied to break it down, he started to flail. I was genuinely concerned until the realization hit me: He was dancing. My soul nearly left the building from the discomfort of witnessing it.

I slowly backed away and rejoined my friends, escaping his gangly limbs that were tripping me out more than I already was. No way I could ever hook up with a guy who danced like that—not even soberly. No thanks.

After I recounted the dance floor disaster to my guy friend, he insisted I give it another shot, reassuring me that dance moves had absolutely no correlation to bedroom skills. It was still a hard no at first, but with each passing sip of my beer my stance softened.

Fuck it, I thought as I ventured back to this dancing noodle. I was in the mood for some dick anyway; I would just have to fast-track our exit out of there.

I made my intentions clear by telling him I wanted to spend the night with him. The surprise on his face made me laugh. Not enough girls are direct nowadays, I guess. He quickly jumped into action, rounding up his friends to head out. As we stumbled our inebriated selves back to his place, he slipped on an icy patch and fell flat on his ass in front of everyone. I felt a bit embarrassed for him—until I remembered his dancing…and nothing could be more embarrassing than that.

The fancy cottage he was staying at was packed with eight guys and six girls, and as soon as we walked in, their stares felt like daggers, as if I had just crashed their exclusive little club. The tension was thick, and I immediately felt out of place. Thankfully, Disco Dan shoved drinks in my hand and ushered me away from the suffocating vibe.

We ended up in a room full of bunk beds, where he clumsily pressed me against the wall. I had to give him credit—he was so confident for someone so awkward. It was such a weird experience, but I remembered the advice from my friend and decided to just go with the flow for the rest of the night.

We were already half-naked when I noticed there was no lock on the door. I pointed it out, and Disco Dan, in true form, walked out in nothing but a towel and announced to his friends, "Don't come in under any circumstances." I'm pretty sure the neighbors heard that too. Smoothness: level zero. But there I was, still hoping for a good lay.

As we continued our uncoordinated make-out session, I overheard one of the girls ask in disbelief, "Are they going to have sex?" *Yes, Felicia, what the fuck do you think adults do when they leave the bar together at 2 a.m.?* I was relieved I didn't have to endure any time with them.

We ended up on the bottom bunk of the closest bed. Disco Dan ate me out with enthusiasm and surprising skill before giving me his nice-sized dick in every different position that he possibly could. He started with the corkscrew. I rested on my hip and forearm at the edge of the bed while he stood on the floor and entered me from behind. He then maneuvered me into the seated wheelbarrow by instructing me to stand and put my hands on the floor in front of me. He sat directly behind me and guided my legs around him as he pumped my ass up and down his shaft. I had never done this position before. It was fun until my arms started to burn from holding myself up. He saw I was getting tired, so he unwrapped my legs from him and guided me back to the wall. He pushed me up against it with slight hesitation. As if he wasn't sure whether I liked being manhandled. I sure did. But not from someone not confident enough to do it. I did like his effort, so I let him continue. He entered me from behind as my cheek pressed against the wall. I felt his grip on my hips tighten when I asked him to fuck me harder. I was glad they had music outside. I never liked to hold back my sounds of gratification. He finally guided me back to the bed, where we both finished in the missionary position.

My friend was right.

After getting dressed, we returned to the living room to discover all eight guys squeezed onto the couch, passed out in upright positions. It was so thoughtful of them to sacrifice their room for their buddy to get laid. While I waited for my friends to pick me up, Disco Dan insisted on serenading me with his guitar. A surprisingly delightful ending to the best awkward sex of my life. Unfortunately, it could never work out between us; his friends were hotter than him.

Moral of the story: Just because you can't dance doesn't mean you shouldn't.

Russian Boy

It was the summer of 2015, and I was as broke as I'd ever been—unemployed and scraping by. So, I took the last $600 from my bank account and joined a sailing club. Seemed like the most reasonable thing to do.

With the membership came lessons, followed by potluck dinners that somehow always turned into all-night parties. Our group of twenty quickly went from strangers to inseparable friends. It was one of the most unexpectedly wholesome experiences of my life.

I wasn't born with any innate desire to sail—I was a certified city dweller. But somehow, life had a way of nudging people toward the water, each for unique reasons. In my class, some were seeking to embrace life more fully, others were celebrating survival after illness. A younger girl wanted to reconnect with childhood memories of boating with her parents, and an older gentleman was just looking for a summer sport to pass the time until ski season rolled around. As for me? I locked eyes with a hot Russian guy during the club tour my friend gave me, and that was all it took. So, there I was.

Our first kiss happened on one of those post-lesson nights. We had just wrapped up a wild dance-off on the picnic tables and wandered out to the dock, where the clubhouse lights couldn't reach us. The night was warm, the stars were out in full force, and the air was thick with the hum of chaos from the party in the distance. We sat side by side, our legs dangling over the edge, when he leaned in to kiss me. But instead of a proper kiss, he only brushed my lips for a split-second before dramatically plummeting into the smelly water. For an instant, he seemed to be drowning—until he realized he could stand up. I hadn't realized this dude was so sloshed. Talk about a buzzkill. I suggested we head back to the party. I wasn't about to make out with a soggy puppy.

Despite our less-than-stellar first kiss, he was hot enough for another chance. So, we made plans to meet up after my already scheduled girls' night that weekend.

As much as I loved my friends, I was ready to leave as soon as I arrived. Thoughts of my upcoming date with Russian Boy kept hip-hopping through my mind as I pretended to enjoy being where I was. After a bunch of cocktails, they finally decided to call it a night. I practically sprinted to the first cab I could find and headed straight for him.

He had to work late, so I met him at his office. He introduced me to his business partner, then asked whether

I liked cocaine. I wasn't expecting this, but I was down. He led me to his car, where we made small talk over warm beers and fresh lines. Our conversation didn't last long because it was late and we were horny.

Once we were naked and ready for each other, he informed me in less than colorful words that his penis had bailed because of the nose party we just had. I assumed he was a seasoned drug user, given the casual manner in which he invited me to partake. I also assumed that because of this, he would be well-acquainted with its effects on his body, but alas, not the case. Recognizing my disappointment, he suggested I lay back so he could go down on me. That I could do. It took a little longer than usual (because, you know, coke) but with help from my fingers, I reached the finish line. It wasn't exactly how I'd envisioned our first time, but hey, an orgasm is an orgasm.

A week later, another opportunity presented itself. What started as a perfect day on the lake quickly morphed into an evening of partying that only the two of us seemed interested in. We had the boathouse to ourselves, along with plenty of party favors and alcohol. Russian Boy had a particular fondness for his nose candy, and I was never one to say no to a good time.

We blasted the music on the speakers and fiercely made out between lines. It was like our own private sex club. We shed our clothes and danced around until we found ourselves on the patio outside. I knelt on the couch while he slowly kissed my neck from behind. He was so sensual. I arched to show him I was ready for his nice solid dick, which was brushing against my back. The lake's symphony served as a sultry backdrop to him slowly filling me up with his member. As our arousal peaked the time between each thrust shortened. When I reached down to touch myself it wasn't long before I felt the pre-orgasm tingle. I whispered that I was close. His hands tightened on my waist as he pulled me onto him harder. I moaned as ecstasy rippled through my whole body. That was enough to make him unleash a slew of Russian profanities as we both climaxed in unison. It was so hot.

We spent the next couple of weeks together until I realized he wasn't just a casual drug user—he was a habitual one. That wasn't the kind of companionship I was looking for. Cocaine is a slippery slope, especially for someone who likes to party as much as I did.

Some party for fun, others to escape. The people you surround yourself with serve as both a reflection of your current self and a compass pointing toward the trajectory of your life.

Tinder Boo

I was twenty-six years old and working as a preschool ski instructor in my hometown. The job brought joy about 20 percent of the time and ice-cold misery the rest. Picture spending an eight-hour shift prying inconsolable kids off the snow. My head ached, my back throbbed, and my toes froze together nearly every day. My sore, chilled body longed for a comforting cuddle, so I decided to try my luck on Tinder. It felt like it was time to dip my toes back into the dating world again.

Doubtful of anything serious coming from a dating app, I swiped with the sole aim of finding a nice warm dick. The sex gods must've been listening because I matched with the perfect prospect just ten minutes later.

He was twenty-nine and looked like a typical bro—jacked arms, handsome boyish face, thick light brown hair, and piercing green eyes. His photo alone heightened my senses, its affect even more impressive when he wasted no time in asking me for my number to see whether we were "compatible." I was intrigued. I liked a man who was direct, but I wasn't handing over my digits just yet. I needed to see what he looked like from all angles. Dating profiles can be deceiving with perfect lighting and carefully chosen shots. I wasn't interested in getting catfished. He offered his social media accounts for a thorough creep session.

His Facebook photos confirmed he was as attractive from every viewpoint, and our ongoing conversation had me laughing out loud. He seemed perfect—genuine, funny, and interested in me—but my curiosity was tempered with skepticism. Finding my ideal guy on Tinder felt too good to be true. There had to be a catch. Maybe he'd just gotten out of a relationship and was looking for a quick rebound? Or maybe he had a weenie voice…or a weenie weenie? I decided to take the plunge anyway. It had been five months since I'd last seen a penis, so really, what was the worst that could happen?

I gave him my number and held my breath when he called for the first time, nervously wondering what his voice would sound like. I was pleasantly surprised—his tone was deep and manly, with no trace of "weenie-ness." We made plans to meet at a restaurant/bar for a classic get-to-know-each-other date. I figured I'd uncover the catch eventually—everything couldn't be this perfect, could it?

He was standing outside the entrance to greet me when I arrived, exactly as tall and handsome as his photos had promised. I couldn't help but feel a surge of satisfaction when I felt the robust strength of his arms wrap around me to say hello.

We sat across from each other in a booth, giving me the perfect chance to study him up close. He was even more attractive in person, but there was something I couldn't quite ignore—he seemed to be having an inner testosterone struggle. His gaze shifted between a subtle primal squint, like a lion sizing up its prey, and a distant stare, as if he wished he were somewhere else. I was simultaneously turned on and off. Was he on something? Steroids? Or was he just naturally high-strung? After a couple of drinks, he finally seemed to relax, enough to keep my interest within the ballpark.

He turned out to be witty and intelligent, and our conversation flowed effortlessly. But as the hour mark of our date approached, he casually suggested I come back to his place. I was caught off guard by his assumption that it would be that simple. When I declined, he shot back, "We don't have to have sex."

"Seriously?" I couldn't help but quip, asking whether he was hoping for a staring contest on his couch instead before excusing myself to the bathroom. Did I have "stupid" written on my forehead? I couldn't help but wonder—was it always this easy for him?

Truth be told, I liked him a lot and definitely wanted to fuck but not after just one hour of getting to know each other. Plus, I wasn't even prepared. I'd purposely left some straggly hairs sporadically around my lady parts so I wouldn't be tempted into anything too soon. No bad first vagina impressions allowed.

When I returned to the table and looked up into his sex-hungry eyes, my body traded sides. Why the hell not? I wasn't going to meet my future husband on Tinder anyway. Who cared whether he thought I was easy? If anything, he was the easy one. The truth was, I probably wouldn't see him again, so there was no point in overthinking a situation that didn't matter. Fuck it. I was going to do him, and I was going to do it right. Mission: Rid Straggly Hairs, activate.

I needed to figure out how to discreetly retrieve my emergency shaver from the glove compartment and get it into a bathroom to tend to my "lady landscape." The only solution that came to mind was suggesting we move to another bar. I needed more time with him, anyway—if we were really going to end up sleeping together, I wanted him to think he'd have to put in a little effort first. He was game.

I walked into the new spot armed and ready. It was another restaurant/bar with live music and a high-spirited older crowd—the atmosphere was perfect. We settled at a table in the dining area and soaked in the good vibes.

We kept talking, and I found myself liking him more with each passing minute. His energy was as intoxicating as the drinks we were sipping. When we stepped outside for a smoke, he pulled me close. The sharp January air swirled around us as he leaned down to kiss me. My whole body melted into his gentle, passionate lips—not at all what I'd expected from someone who seemed like a raging sex beast.

Still not quite ready to call it a night, we ordered another round. As we waited, an Oasis song ("Wonderwall") filled the air, and the whole place erupted in song. Without missing a beat, Tinder Boo jumped up and started dancing in the middle of the dining area, where everyone was seated. I was on my feet before he could even extend his hand. I wasn't about to turn down an impromptu dance-off! He looked genuinely surprised that I'd joined in without hesitation. This guy had no idea who he was dealing with. And there we were, hand in hand, spinning around in the back of a restaurant filled with people three times our age. I watched the hungry look in his eyes finally soften into something lighter. In that moment, there was nowhere in the world I wanted to be more.

I sensed that we were going to leave soon, so I excused myself to the restroom. As I stepped inside, I had no clue he was right behind me—until, in one swift motion, he spun me around and swept me off my feet. He effortlessly held me up as I straddled him and kissed me deeply. The raunchy bathroom faded away, and I almost let him take me right there. However, I knew I had to play my cards right if I wanted him to call me back after this night. I gently pushed him away so I could trim my hedges in secret. Mission complete.

He led me to the basement of his parents' house, where he resided. His kisses had shifted to a different intensity than earlier, as if he had morphed back into the ravenous lion from the beginning of the night. I had to firmly instruct him to calm the fuck down when he began roughly removing my clothes. "This is a marathon, not a sprint." He slowed his pace and stuck his face in my nicely shaved vagina. Success.

I was hot and ready. He was a lion and I his lioness. I purred as he gave me his thick cock and submitted to wherever his rock-hard arms placed me. We were on the carpeted floor when he paused to pick up his belt. He quickly told me not to worry when he saw the look on my face. I had no idea where this was going. He directed me to get on all fours in front of him and traced the belt up and down my back. He folded it in the middle and slapped my ass with it sharply before buckling it loosely around my waist. He held onto it with both hands as he placed himself inside of me and used it to rein me in roughly each time he thrusted. The beast I knew he'd been subduing all night was unleashed. I'm pretty sure the noises of pleasure from my mouth resembled some sort of animal but I couldn't hold anything in. He fucked me hard and finished after I did with one last growl. Every nerve ending in my body quivered with gratification. I was in love.

I wasn't sure whether he felt the same so I hid my feelings by refraining from looking at him as we lay there catching our breath. I was about to get up and leave when he turned to me and asked me to spend the night. I couldn't stop the oxygen from getting sucked out of me. This meant he liked me more than a one-night stand and maybe just as much as I liked him. It was the exact scenario I was hoping for. As much as I wanted to fall asleep in his arms, I knew I had to decline. He would want me more if he missed me, so I didn't want to move right into the sleepover phase of the relationship. Plus, I didn't want to meet the parents with a raging hangover.

I did, however, meet the parents the next week. He invited me over and dragged me into the living room with golden retriever energy to introduce me to them. They were just as excited to meet me. My heart was so happy.

Tinder Boy and I were inseparable for six incredible, sex-filled months. We couldn't get enough of each other. Even after hanging out all day we would talk on the phone all night. I was never bored or questioned whether this was true love. He was the only person who mattered in any room we were in, the only man I'd ever made love to. He was everything I had been searching for and all I'd ever dreamed of in human form. We were going to spend the rest our existence together...or so I thought. I was beyond devastated to find out it was all a lie. Everything. He was a cheating, narcissistic sociopath with major drug issues and an insatiable sex drive that he satisfied with multiple women over our time together. That was the catch.

When I ended things, he cried in my arms, vowing to do whatever it took to get me back. Despite knowing he wasn't a good person, my love for who I believed he could be made me desperately yearn for his return. I whispered and yelled his name to the stars hoping they'd lead him back to me. Fortunately, his attempts at redemption were so pathetically weak that I blocked him shortly after. My heart was obliterated. He sucked all the life out of me, and I'd given him the straw. I felt so dumb. I had never experienced such cruelty before.

Looking back, the red flags were there, but I chose to overlook them. I wanted to be an easygoing girlfriend as he navigated what I thought was his journey of self-discovery. It was all a lie. I hope he paid for every tear that I shed. I would not wish such a soul-crushing experience on anyone.

> *The right person will ensure your heart doesn't ache for them.*

Fortunate Fella

The breakup with Tinder Boo was somewhat softened by my new job in California, a locale far removed from any place I had ever been.

I was hired as a tour leader for adventure vacations, a role that involved guiding people from all around the world on road trips across North America. It was an absolute dream job. My responsibility highlights involved venturing to the best parts of different cities, exploring the beautiful national parks, and camping under the stars every night. I literally got to chaperone my ideal vacation over and over for seven months. I would've done it for free.

After finishing my two-week training, I had some free time before my inaugural trip. Taking advantage of the break, I decided to attend the Enchanted Forest Gathering—a conscious living festival focused on art, dance, music, and personal growth. The days were filled with workshops designed to empower, enlighten, and entertain while the nights featured DJ performances and other sensory experiences. Though none of my colleagues were down to join me, I knew I'd meet new people once I got there. Besides, it seemed like the perfect place for my curious spirit to try acid for the first time—or maybe just get laid. Either would do.

I arrived on the final day, surrounded by those who seemed to have already found their tribes. I, however, remained unbothered. My confidence and self-worth had matured over time, and I had grown comfortable in my own company. I trusted that the right connections would come when ready.

I spent the morning weaving through crowds of naked hippie families, dancing solo and hopping between various workshops while waiting for the one I was really excited about—the Lap Dancing 101 class at 1 p.m. My inner stripper had been eagerly anticipating this since I saw it on the schedule. I arrived early to make sure I got a good partner—one I'd actually want to straddle. I'm open-minded, but there are some laps I'd rather not sit on.

I settled into the designated area and quickly spotted the Fortunate Fella two feet to my left. While his wiry, untamed beard didn't particularly float my boat, everything else about him was appealing. Plus, he didn't appear to be tripping balls like most of the people around, so I knew we would be a good match. Grateful to the universe, I confidently scooted over to introduce myself. He was friendly and visibly stoked when I asked him to be my partner for the class. Thank God he said yes because just as we were about to begin, a disheveled, cracked-out Russell

Brand lookalike swaggered up to me as though we shared some cosmic, undeniable connection that made us automatic playmates. Just no.

What followed was probably the most absurd thirty minutes of my life. A tall, slender instructor had us flopping around in synchronized circles with our partners, alternating sitting on each other's laps. I had come ready to gyrate my booty on some lucky gent, but instead, I was being told to move like an inflatable tube man in a windstorm. It was then that I realized I was way too sober for this. Everyone else, except for Fortunate Fella and me, were definitely in another dimension. So, when the instructor's back was turned, we made our exit. Enough was enough.

We headed over to the food trucks to grab some lunch as we continued to get to know each other. I nearly choked on my drink when he casually mentioned his age. This kid was eighteen! Not even legal drinking age. I almost died inside. He looked so much more mature than that; I was honestly shocked.

If I hadn't just ended things with the guy I thought I'd spend forever with, I probably would've bolted. But honestly? I wanted the D, so *fuck it*. I hadn't been able to get my hands on any LSD, so screwing him would be the next best thing.

After we finished eating, he led me to the cuddle tent. Fortunate Fella was nothing if not direct. The age gap and his unruly beard quickly faded from my mind as he took the lead, kissing and holding me in a way that soothed my bruised heart. It felt almost sweet...until he started dry-humping me aggressively. I love a bit of PDA, but that was a hard pass. I suggested we head somewhere more private, and with a charming nod, he led me to his tent.

When I took his pants off I was pleasantly surprised by his big cock. I placed my chest on his and tilted my pelvis up so he could guide himself inside. I was very impressed with the care he took in making sure I could handle it. He continued slowly, stopping only to have me sit back enough for him to grab my breasts and suck on my nipples. It was clearly not this young man's first rodeo. He was well-versed in how to pleasure a woman. I sat upright and gave him a little ride before deciding that I was ready to come. I leaned forward and whispered for him to fuck me slowly as I touched myself, finishing almost immediately with moans that echoed outside the thin tent walls.

Although I was ready to enjoy the festival I wanted him to finish as well. My knees were hurting from our position, so I hopped off and had him give it to me while on my back. Boy did he give it. This boy did not stop. I asked him if he was tired multiple times, hoping he was ready to shoot his load, but he responded by enthusiastically increasing the velocity of his thrusts. He finished almost three hours after we started. *Three hours of missionary sex in a tent!* I couldn't believe it. That had to be a record somewhere. Was I a cougar now?

We emerged from our enclosure into a mesmerizing nighttime scene. A neon glow from the surrounding art installations cast a surreal radiance over everything, alongside a cascade of twinkling tree lights. It was magical. Hand in hand, we wandered down a winding path to a silent disco, where we lost ourselves in the rhythm of the night as we danced together. Our evening ended in a communal sleeping tent, where we curled up under a blanket, tangled in each other's warmth as a band serenaded us into dreamland with a euphoric symphony. It was one of those rare moments where everything felt right in my life. My empty heart was filled.

I raced back to my workplace before the sun came up. It was a three-hour drive and I had to make it there by 8 a.m. The exhilarating weekend still pulsed through me. I was actually grateful that no one I'd invited came with me. Experiencing something of this magnitude solo had been eye-opening. It was as if I'd unlocked a new level of freedom—realizing that I was capable of anything, as long as I wasn't afraid to do it alone.

Life doesn't always unfold as you expect; sometimes it's even better.

Drive-By Guy

My job continued to be the perfect post-breakup distraction. I was two months in and selected to lead tours in Western Canada—a coveted assignment that every tour leader dreamed of. Our office was based in the heart of Vancouver, and I was ecstatic to explore my new playground. I decided that I wanted a tan to accompany me as I galivanted around the city so I rallied my favorite coworker and dragged her to Wreck Beach. A clothing-optional place where I could ensure a tan with no lines. Those wouldn't look good in the photos I planned to post to show off my fabulous adventures on social media.

As we neared the entrance, a guy driving by pulled over to ask for directions. Without missing a beat, I told him that wherever he was headed wouldn't be as fun as where we were going, so he might as well join us. He agreed.

It was my first time at a nude beach so I took everything in slowly as I surveyed the scene. The view was very interesting. Clusters of people were scattered about. Some in small groups and completely nude, and others in larger groups with varying degrees of clothing. My favorite part had to be the very old men running around playing an absurdly intense game of frisbee as their willys flopped freely in the wind. I decided to equally embrace the experience and stripped down to nothing. As I lay back to crisp my body, a flamboyant naked man came by selling alcoholic freeze pops. I was sold.

Drive-By Guy clearly wanted to stick around as much as I did, so when my coworker called it quits we decided to hang back. He regaled me with stories of music festival orgies, his raging sex life, and his current polyamorous relationships. While he wasn't exactly a sight to behold, I found myself intrigued by his wealth of sexual experiences. So, I decided to invite him to my hotel for a spin.

We took a shower separately and then reconvened on the bed. The little connection I thought we had fizzled as soon as I smelled his dragon breath creeping through his sand castle-textured lips. I swerved my head a side to kiss his neck as his supposedly experienced hands groped me like a virgin. It was awful.

He thrusted inside of me emotionlessly. It felt like I was being fucked by a robot with a sneering face. Yes, he was sneering the whole time. I wasn't sure if that was just his sex face or self-pride for coercing me to sleep with him. It was by far the worst sex I had ever experienced.

I faked an orgasm to make this mentally painful encounter end. How could someone in three non-monogamous partnerships and loads of sexual experience under their belt be this bad? Who in their right mind would entertain any type of relationship with someone so off-putting? Had he spent the whole afternoon lying about everything? I could not wrap my head around it.

I could only attribute my current state of affairs to those damn spiked freeze pops. They allowed me to let his cunning stories whisper pleasure to my curious, sexual desires. Nothing else connected us other than the idea of a good lay.

The more you drink,
the less you think.

Cloud-Snatcher

A week had passed since my Drive-By Guy encounter. The unsatisfying experience made me nostalgic for my ex. I missed the way he fucked me. I knew I couldn't continue down the rabbit hole of my memories of him, so off to the bar I went. It was definitely a tequila night.

I staggered back to my hotel, caught somewhere between tipsy and full-on hammered. Before heading up to my room, I figured I'd stop by the smoking area for a quick nicotine fix. A gnarly man and pretty girl were there, and it was painfully obvious he was head over heels for her yet trapped in the friend zone. Despite the obvious tension, they welcomed me like an old buddy. I was even more delighted when they invited me to their room to do cocaine.

I only stuck around for a couple lines—as much as I was buzzing, I had work in a few hours and didn't want to risk the job I actually cared about. We agreed to keep the party going the next night instead.

I flew through my to-do list the next day, eager to free up my evening for round two with my new friends. After quickly devouring a peanut butter and jelly sandwich for dinner—because, despite a wealth of experience, I was still very broke—I made my way to their room.

They greeted me with a monstrous line as soon as I entered. The gnarly man, clearly aware of my financial situation, insisted I'd be doing them a solid by helping them polish off their stash before they left town. I remember thinking how lucky I was to find such generous friends. We filled our noses greedily before deciding to continue our party at a strip club.

The venue was packed with hot, jacked biker dudes and sexy dancers. I was soaring. I couldn't decide which sex I wanted more, and for a moment, I wasn't sure whether my thoughts about exploring something with a woman were because I was gay or just curious. My confusion resolved itself the second my eyes landed on the rugged, tattooed, tough-looking guy sitting at the table next to us. Yep, definitely straight.

One thing about free drugs: You've got to keep the people sharing them with you entertained—especially if you want to keep the supply coming. Gnarly Man was chill, but Pretty Girl would not stop talking. Seriously, we couldn't go ten seconds without her rambling on about some pointless nonsense. She was killing my vibe. Just as I was plotting my escape, she mentioned her "boy toy" was nearby. I quickly convinced her that meeting up with him was definitely the best idea ever. And thank God, she bought it. Finally, we were free to finish off the rest of Gnarly Man's stash with boobs, biker dudes, and peace.

We had such a blast getting fucked up together that once the drugs ran out, we decided to grab some food to end our night.

We weren't exactly shocked to find the diner packed when we arrived—the Google reviews had been off the charts, so it was bound to be busy. We decided to wait outside until a table opened up. While we chatted, I casually glanced through the window and locked eyes with a handsome guy sitting at the bar. There was an instant connection and I knew I had to have him. I shared my intentions with Gnarly Man, who gave me his blessing, and I confidently made my way into the diner. But just as quickly as my excitement rose, it deflated. Out of nowhere, a girl appeared and slid into the seat next to him. *That was my seat!* I felt my blood pressure raise as I walked past them, pretending to head to the restroom, which, conveniently, was in that direction.

I stared at myself in the mirror, silently seeking guidance. Time was of the essence; their conversation had to be cut short if I wanted to make my move. After a deep breath and quick little pep talk, I grabbed my huge cojones and made my way over. He was mine.

They were deep in conversation when I tapped him on the shoulder and greeted him with an overly familiar, "Heyyy!"—like we were long-lost pals. They both turned to look at me, and I asked, "Do you remember me from that party last year?" He gave me a confused look and shook his head, clearly not recognizing what was happening. I paused to give him a second to process, then turned to the girl beside him and asked, "Are you his girlfriend?" She quickly answered, "No.'

I shifted my attention back to him, casually saying, "I finally got a new phone and lost all my numbers—what was yours again?" He looked completely taken aback, as did the girl and the people at the bar listening in. The expressions around us, ranging from shock to amusement, were priceless; the few struggling to hold back laughter only fueled my adrenaline. I was always up for putting on a show. My phone was out and ready as he, still stunned, slowly gave me his number. The girl next to him wasn't thrilled, but honestly, I wasn't too concerned—he was mine first.

I made my way back to Gnarly Man, who was waiting for me outside. As I walked away, I could feel the girl's furious gaze burning into my back through the window, so I decided it was best to leave the place altogether.

As soon as I hopped in the cab, I texted him. He replied almost instantly, asking if he could come over. I liked that he matched my forwardness.

Half an hour later, I opened the door to my hotel room and was met with a giant. Holy daddy long legs, he was tall—six-foot-seven, to be exact. His face was still cute, but he looked much better sitting down. The intoxicants had definitely run their course.

We exchanged a few words that neither of us really cared about, then got straight down to business.

He kissed me passionately as we took off our clothes. The thought of each other had warmed us up enough to breeze through foreplay. His penis wasn't small, but I thought it would be bigger for how huge he was. Still, he knew how to work it very well. This surprised me because I assumed someone that tall wouldn't have any coordination. I stopped the inner dialogue to enjoy the entire six minutes it lasted.

After he finished he started a full-on "get to know you" conversation as I sat there in disbelief. All hot and bothered I asked if he could go again, and he said no because he was drunk. Not seeing any issue in the fact that I hadn't orgasmed. After all of that build-up, this was it? I made him suck on my nipple as I rubbed one out. How annoying. What was even more annoying was that he had no intention of leaving. He tried to cuddle me to sleep until I moved to the other bed to get away.

I woke up in the morning to him asking whether I would like to fuck as he crept into the bed with me. I absolutely did not want to and said I was too tired to move. He did not take the hint. Cloud-Snatcher excitedly reassured me that he would do all the work. A little part inside thought that maybe he was going to make up for the shitty dick-down he gave me the previous night. But no, this beanstalk wriggled inside and on top of me for another six minutes and then turned over to sleep right after he finished. I was pissed. He needed to leave.

I got up and started slamming drawers and doors, trying to wake up the snoring skyscraper. Two hours later, he finally left—though not before lingering at the door, clearly hoping for more than my flat "Bye." No. Fuck you. I was done with Vancouver boys.

I made some random girl feel awful over this waste of time—all because I was trying to fill the void left by my ex. Honestly, I was more disappointed in myself than any D. Definitely not my finest moment.

A broken heart sometimes makes you not a very nice person. Be aware of your power to destroy—and choose not to.

Flash

My seasonal gig as an adventure tour leader was coming to an end, and I was kicking off my final trip in none other than Las Vegas—a destination I fully intended to take advantage of. The first night was chaos. I partied hard, only to face the consequences the next day. I finally rolled out of bed at the ungodly hour of 3 p.m., my empty stomach staging a full-blown rebellion. As I dragged myself down Fremont Street in search of food, a guy selling skincare products stopped me. I gave a polite smile and tried to brush him off, but he wasn't having it. He persisted until my last nerve was rattled. I snapped, telling him I was hungover and starving. "Unless you plan to buy me food, I'm not interested in talking," I said. He just nodded and followed me to a restaurant. That was a plot twist.

Our lunch was surprisingly pleasant, and I realized that he was actually attractive after the hanger subsided, of course. We parted ways after making plans for dinner later that evening. Only in Vegas, right?

He pulled up in a fancy Mercedes and swept me away to an upscale restaurant. We ate, laughed, and drank—honestly, I couldn't believe I'd scored two free meals in one day. Jackpot! As we wrapped up, he insisted he "really" wanted to give me a massage at his place. Now, let's be real—no guy wants to massage a female and call it a night. But as luck would have it, I was feeling…a little adventurous that day.

We arrived at his bedroom in no time. He administered the weakest thirty-second massage before deciding that it was fuck time. Thirty seconds after he stuck it in he started convulsing on top of me. I legitimately thought he was having a seizure. He was making a sound like a cartoon character getting electrocuted. I had no idea what was going on. It all happened in a flash. After he finished spazzing out he rolled over and lay beside me. That's when it dawned on me: He had just come.

It took everything inside of me not to cry-laugh. I had never experienced something so strange. I gulped down the howl as he started kissing me tenderly and calling me sweetheart in his language. He then caressed me while looking deeply into my eyes. I was so disoriented. This was too weird. I had to leave before he tried to make me his wife.

It was another night of me and my hand.

I wondered whether I would ever have good sex again. Was an orgasm with the help of a man too much to ask? The past couple of encounters had been beyond disappointing. Why did men think it was okay to forget about a woman's pleasure? Prematurely ejaculating would be less awkward if the situation was handled properly afterward.

Sex should always be a mutually fulfilling experience, not a one-sided transaction.

Bar Master

I'd known Bar Master for a solid eight years before anything even remotely sexual unfolded between us. Our paths first crossed at the banquet hall where I started working at nineteen. He was the suave, confident bartender in his thirties, always slipping me drinks when I asked. With a twinkle in his eye and a swagger in his step, he quickly became one of my favorite people. We had countless deep conversations and would close out every bar we visited after work. He was one of my favorite human beings. Little did I know, that twinkle was actually him mentally undressing me. Dirty man!

After my season as a tour leader ended, I returned to my old stomping grounds. It had been a while, and I was long overdue for a reunion with all my friends. Bar Master was the first on my list.

We met at the arena where his boat was docked. Although we had planned to take a ride around the lake, the dangerously choppy waters led us to decide on a hike instead. As he drove us to the trailhead, we slipped into easy conversation, just like the old days. At that moment, there was still no thought of sex on my mind.

After a scenic hike, we decided to continue our reunion with a bar crawl back to my car. We kicked things off with our usual routine—shots of Jameson followed by beers. By the second bar, I couldn't help but notice his perfectly styled salt-and-pepper hair. By the time we hit the third bar, I found myself admiring his handsome features even more. It wasn't until the fourth bar that it hit me like a ton of bricks—I had been secretly fantasizing about being with an older man for a while, and here he was, a silver fox right in front of me. The opportunity had been staring me in the face the whole time. How had I not seen it sooner?

As we closed out the last bar, the decision was made to continue the party on his boat—after all, that was the original plan. When we arrived, he fixed me another drink and reassured me that I didn't need to worry about driving home. We were both pretty buzzed by then. He was always respectful, so I knew if anything was going to happen, I'd have to take the lead. I looked up at him coyly and asked, "Are you going to kiss me or not?" Without hesitation, his lips met mine. The directness fanned the spark within me. The soft sounds of the water and the gentle bumping of the boats against their moorings added to the romantic atmosphere. Excitedly, I followed him down to the sleeping quarters.

He was *extra* large, rough, and made sure to do everything that pleased me. I was ravenous for more friction when he placed me on top. In a fit of passionate aggression, I impulsively slapped him in the face. To my surprise, he swiftly returned the gesture. It wasn't forceful, but it was a first for me, and strangely, I didn't hate it. He flashed a sly smile as he watched the emotions run across my face.

As I continued to ride, he placed one of his big hands firmly around my neck, applying pressure enough to thrill me without restricting my breath. This unfamiliar pain and pleasure mix aroused me differently than I'd ever been aroused before.

After watching me enjoy this moment for a couple of minutes, he commanded me to my stomach. From the corners of the bed, he retrieved straps and carefully fastened them around my wrists and ankles so that my body was completely stretched to its limits. He told me to trust him as I felt the restraints hold me in place, and I did. He caressed my body gently as he traced his tongue all the way down my back. I surrendered to his mouth as he spread my ass and ventured inside with his experienced movements. I saw his hand grab my lace thong out of the corner of my eye as he traced his way back up to my neck. As I was about to ask him what he was doing he gently wrapped my underwear around my neck and tightened it slowly as he positioned himself at my inviting entrance. He then served me with his enormous penis until I culminated in a fit of euphoria. Every nerve ending tingled in delight. Finally, my good sex drought was over.

In the delicate dance between friendship and intimacy, trust is the step that keeps everything in balance.

Girlfriend

I had a girlfriend whom I considered my sexual soul sister. We met five years earlier in a dingy after-hours club's basement, and I instantly adored her. She was beautiful, bubbly, kind, and hilarious—the kind of person who made you feel comfortable in any situation.

I always looked forward to hanging out with her because of all the laughter we shared, often at our own expense. Our love lives were both a hot mess. We joked that we should just date each other, or at least have a threesome together.

The joke turned real when she sent me a picture of her ridiculously hot new fuck boy while I was throwing back shots at a wedding reception. My senses were already buzzing from the atmosphere and the alcohol, so when her invite to join came through—I ordered an Uber right away.

I tried to be subtle as I entered her living room, but it was hard to contain my desire. Girlfriend looked incredibly sexy in a tight leather outfit standing over her super-hot shirtless boy toy who had his washboard abs on full display. I was so turned on.

She handed me a fruity cocktail and told me to get aquatinted with Fuck Boy as she picked out a playlist to set the mood. I wasn't too interested in formalities so I sat beside him and placed my lips on his to say hello. I could tell he was equally as excited for this adventure.

We made out until Girlfriend joined us on the couch. I focused my attention on her as Fuck Boy sat back and watched us kiss in front of him. Her lips were soft and her sweet breath reminiscent of the drink she gave me.

Fuck Boy's hardness pressed between us as we caressed him over his clothes. When we were ready to include him, Girlfriend worked on getting his pants off while I kissed and nibbled his neck. His eyes rolled back in bliss as I watched Girlfriend skillfully take the tip of his pretty joystick into her mouth and begin to suck. I wanted to be closer to her soft lips so I joined her. He pulsated as we licked his shaft in unison. It was so hot.

She whispered that she wanted to watch me fuck him so I sensually slid my body up against his as she placed his hard manhood inside of me. I sank into him and gently bounced as he filled me up. Fuck Boy extended his hand to caress Girlfriend's clit while I touched my own. This was my first time experiencing a woman so intimately. Witnessing her being pleasured as I indulged in my own was unexpectedly exhilarating—a newfound aspect of sensuality I never anticipated enjoying as much as I did.

We stopped in the kitchen on our way to the bedroom. Fuck Boy finally took some initiative and ordered us to bend over the counter. Assertiveness always aroused me. He fucked me while simultaneously fingering Girlfriend, then switched to give her some of his dick. It felt like a porno you would watch without skipping to final moments.

I knew I was on the verge of climaxing when we finally made it to the room so I instructed Fuck Boy to continue fucking Girlfriend. She deserved all the attention for orchestrating this beautiful experience anyway. He laid her on her back and took her aggressively. I watched intently as I rubbed her clit with my left hand and touched myself with my right. She finished with a sensual moan.

It was finally my turn and I was ready to let out everything I'd been holding back. He flipped me onto my stomach with his nice strong arms and gripped my hips as he pulled me back onto him. I could feel his grasp intensify as he reveled in the sensation of being inside me. I was completely lost in the moment until I realized that my friend had slipped away

So there I was, in the midst of being pounded by this magnificent man, with my friend who initially invited me nowhere in sight. I was very confused. I told him to stop so we could figure out what was going on. This was her boy toy and I didn't feel right having sex with him without her there. We found her outside smoking and I knew right away that sexy time was over. She reassured us she was fine, but I could sense her discomfort. My friendship with her outweighed any fleeting pleasure from a fuck boy. So I decided to leave and let them have their space.

Me and Girlfriend still laugh about it to this day. It was a fun night and a great first time experience for both of us. Despite how it concluded.

There's an unspoken friendship code that holds more significance than getting some dick. When exploring your sexuality with someone you care about, it's important for everyone involved to act with respect and consideration. It's not fun unless it's fun for everyone.

Captain Try Too Hard

At the tender age of twenty-seven I decided to move to Vegas to become a stripper. I figured I had a couple more years of perky boobs so I might as well make the most of them. Plus I had a head full of steamy fantasies and a bank account emptier than a desert highway. Two birds, one stone.

I met Captain Try Too Hard on a twerk night. At first, I wasn't interested in engaging with him—he gave off the typical vibe of the "I don't spend money at strip clubs" guy. You know the type: an air of superiority that often matches their looks. Even baby strippers like me can spot and avoid them without a second thought. I only approached him because, frankly, there wasn't any other options—the club was dead.

I strolled up and plopped my booty down on his lap. His first words? "You like it rough and would love my big dick." I rolled my eyes up to silently ask for patience. Good ice breaker, bro. What sexually active woman doesn't like a nice pounding from a nice dick? You just don't have to say it within the first sentence of meeting someone. Anyway, beyond his constant alpha male declarations, he was surprisingly decent to chat with.

After thirty minutes of lively banter, I finally convinced his cheap ass to splurge on a $20 lap dance. The VIP rooms were where the big dollars were made but I would take something over nothing.

I looked into his eyes and gently smiled as I unclipped my bra and straddled him. Surprisingly, he didn't try to aggressively grope me as I thought he would after all his shit talking about rough sex. While gyrating to the music I ran my hands up the side of my body to my breasts. After a little squeeze I leaned forward to immerse his face in my cleavage. I'm not saying that I was born to be a stripper but it definitely came naturally to me. I felt him loosen up as I sensually ran my fingers along the back of his neck. I placed my lips close to his ears and asked if he liked that with a whisper. He shivered ever so slightly as goosebumps rippled across his skin. When the song finished I knew he wanted more of me.

I gave him my number after he demanded it. Although his alpha wannabe schtick was very off-putting, I was hopeful for a pounding from the nice big dick he wouldn't shut up about. He called to arrange a meetup two days later.

We rendezvoused at the casino next to his condo a couple of hours later, and almost immediately, he began his campaign to lure me back to his place. Turns out, Captain

Try Too Hard "didn't do dates." I promptly informed him that regardless of my job description, I wasn't about to run into someone's bed without some effort on their part. So, I guided him to the lobby bar where he could buy me drinks while we chatted until I was ready. I was a classy hoe.

He observed me as I sipped my vodka, mentioning his vow of sobriety. I found this admirable considering he lived in the heart of Sin City. After my second drink he delved into a monologue about what an alpha man was and how he embodied it until I abruptly changed the subject. I wasn't on the clock and there was no way I was going to pretend to like the asinine things coming out of his mouth on my day off. Thankfully he was intelligent on other subjects. By the time I finished my third drink I was primed for action.

My anticipation for this promised domination and potential love affair escalated as we made our way to his place. I remember thinking how perfect it would be to have a fuck buddy to experience Vegas with. He walked straight into his room as soon as we entered. Despite feeling like I might be rushing into things I followed.

He clumsily pulled me in to make out. His stubbly beard pricking me as he kissed me hungrily. It wasn't the nicest sensation, but it wasn't unbearable either. Once my clothes were off, he placed his hands under my armpits and shakily lifted me up like in the scene from *The Lion King* in which Mufasa raises Simba to show him to the animal kingdom. I wasn't sure where he was going with this so I stayed somewhat limp as he held me there for three unsteady seconds before using every last ounce of his strength to toss me onto the bed. His awkward attempt to seductively manhandle me was so pathetic that any desire I felt for him quickly dissipated.

As he unwrapped the condom, I lay there hoping that the promised "big penis" would erase the previous sixty seconds from the night. When he climbed on top, I eagerly reached down to feel what he had been raving about, only to have my hand wrap around it twice. *What...the...fuck?!?* I was pissed. I couldn't believe that someone with whom I had openly made a plan to sleep with would spend so much time exaggerating the size of their dick, as if I was never going to see it. Did he think he could gaslight me into believing it was big? This man-child was thirty-seven years old. Didn't he have enough experience to know that you don't need a huge penis for a girl to like you? I was speechless. I really thought he was somewhat intelligent.

I let him penetrate me for a disappointing fifteen minutes of questioning whether it was in or not. I couldn't even muster the enthusiasm to give myself a hand. Here I was thinking that guys stop lying to sleep with you after a certain age. Boy, was I wrong. I would never speak to this guy again.

A real man needs no grand declarations.

McDreamy

It had been five months since I'd last seen a penis—a much-needed break after my stupid encounter with Captain Try Too Hard. Contrary to popular belief, strippers don't have as much sex as people think. Many of my industry friends were asexual, married, lesbians, or just working their way through school. We weren't there for the sex; it was all about the money.

It was a busy Saturday at the club, and I hadn't stopped moving since I arrived three hours earlier. I was on fire—money was flowing from everyone I spent time with, and my financial worries felt like distant memories. I was riding high on life. Deciding to take a quick break, I caught up with my friend Cherry, whom I hadn't seen all night. As we chatted, a strange tingling sensation crept up the back of my neck, putting me on alert. Before I could process it, an invisible force seemed to turn me around to face the very embodiment of my dream man approaching. It was like watching an angel descend—his body framed in a heavenly glow, lit by the lights behind him. He was ruggedly handsome, with the perfect amount of facial hair that accentuated his chiseled jawline. I forgot to breathe as my eyes traced around his dark hair and face. He was mesmerizing. That invisible force pushed me directly into his path, and before I knew it, my hand was on his muscular chest, stopping him from walking by. Up close, he was even more stunning. There was no way he was leaving without a sexy dance. After a quick hello, he wrapped his strong arms around Cherry and me, and we led him straight to the VIP room for an hour of fun.

The host collected our payment and directed us to a booth in the corner to begin our time. Almost immediately after exchanging names, McDreamy surprised us by pulling down his pants to proudly display his manhood, exclaiming, "See? Not bad." We burst into laughter as we scrambled to help him put himself away. The club was incredibly strict, with cameras in every corner. Even though it was a VIP room no sexual services or nudity was allowed. Topless dances only. Anyone caught breaking these rules was fired immediately.

We took our bras off and began our synchronous sensual seduction. It wasn't the first time that my girlfriend and I had worked together, and we had a little routine. We each took a side of his lap and traced our hands provocatively along his chest and shoulders. She had long nails so while she worked her way up his neck to his head I turned around and slid my booty onto his lap. I could feel his excitement. After I grinded slowly to the music, Cherry and I switched positions. By this time it was very apparent that McDreamy was only interested in me. Cherry didn't mind, as he wasn't her type and would be paid for the hour regardless. She graciously moved to the side so that we could continue without her.

Our sexy dance escalated into a full-on make-out session. I knew I could lose my job for this but I couldn't stop myself. I wanted him so badly. He swiftly removed his shirt, revealing his flawless body, and before I knew it, he effortlessly lifted me and laid me on my back. He moved my lingerie to the side and brought his face down to pleasure me with his tongue. My shock mingled with excitement. It all happened so fast that I didn't even have time to hope that no one was monitoring the cameras. I had never allowed anyone to get dirty with me at work, but I couldn't resist him. I wanted him to take me right there. Cherry glanced over and laughed a few times, but remained on the lookout for any roaming host. She was the best.

I didn't let him finish me off because I wouldn't have been able to hold in my sounds of gratification. So we exchanged numbers and arranged to meet up the following day.

This handsome beautiful man showed up to my door in a plaid button-down and cowboy boots. I damn near fainted. There is nothing like a rugged-looking jacked man in country attire. It was my new obsession.

We both stripped on our way to the bedroom where he threw me on the bed with ease. He passionately pressed his lips against mine before making a trail of kisses down to where he left off the previous night. His experienced tongue traced the outside of my flower before gripping my waist with his big, strong hands and burying his face inside. I was on cloud nine.

When he was satisfied with his work he kissed me all the way up until his perfect penis was right outside my inviting body. I gasped as he slowly pushed himself inside. He took his time to pick up the pace until he was delivering the pounding we both wanted. I held on to his rock-hard arms as beads of sweat started to form on his forehead. I could not get enough of this flawless man. The tickle of an orgasm creeped in so quickly that I succumbed before I could stop myself. He continued to give it to me until I finished then rolled me on top of him to catch his breath. My legs were too weak to do anything so he caressed my lips with his as he readied himself to climax. He gave me one more minute of his rock-hard dick from under me and released with a growl that almost sent me into another dimension of bliss.

He was good.

While he was a perfect gentleman before, during, and after our encounter, I knew he didn't see me as anything more than a Vegas adventure. It was the price I had to pay for where I lived and the profession I chose.

The way you decide to live your life is a form of art. Recognize the difference between those who appreciate it and those who don't.

Blondie

As I made my usual rounds at work, I spotted a stylish looking fella standing at the bar alone. He was tall and blonde and exuded a cheerful confidence—I was intrigued. The past few shifts had been filled with people dumping their emotional baggage on me for pennies instead of buying dances. I was done with that. Tonight, it was big-dollar time.

We had a genuine, down-to-earth conversation, and I could tell he was starting to warm up to me. But when I mentioned a dance in the VIP room, he hesitated. I knew I had to act fast before he tried to lowball me with a cheap floor lap dance, so I promised him my number if he agreed. Truth be told, I would've given it to him anyway, but I had bills to pay.

I loved getting paid to dance for someone I actually liked. When our hour together ended, we made plans to hit up a nightclub the next evening. I was definitely excited

The next day, butterflies fluttered in my stomach as I

walked to our meeting spot outside of the club. But the moment I saw him, they vanished. I forgot to take into consideration how much better people looked in the dim lighting of my job. I definitely wasn't interested in sitting on his penis. Still, I decided to stay for a couple of drinks. I couldn't just go home after all the time I'd spent on my hair and makeup. Plus, maybe a little alcohol would change my perspective.

I was completely hammered within twenty minutes. The guilt of planning on ditching him was gnawing at me; he was such a nice person, but I was still not attracted to him. He wasn't ugly, just not as good-looking as I had initially thought. I didn't want to leave him high and dry so I blurted out while we were dancing that I had just gotten my period and couldn't have sex. He stopped and stared me straight in the eye and said, "I'm a man, I don't give a shit. Are you serious or are you just lying to me?" Talk about a sudden change of events. His directness spoke right to my woman parts. Waking them from the dry desert they rested in. However, I panicked and swore up and down that "I definitely had my period and would never lie about it." *Crap.*

I walked away kicking myself for fucking up so badly. I really wanted him now! I couldn't possibly go back and tell him that I had lied. Or could I?

Well I did.

I marched back up to him and spun a story about how I didn't want to sleep with someone I'd never see or talk to again. He bought it, assuring me it wasn't going to be like that. We decided to leave together right away. I was so drunk that I passed out in the cab, sprawled across him in the back seat.

I woke up abruptly when we pulled up to the hotel, and an overwhelming craving for fries hit me. It was a life-or-death situation—just kidding; maybe more like a fries-or-no-sex situation. He probably thought I was joking, because as soon as we entered his room, he tried to make a move. But I stood my ground and told him, "No fries, no love." With a sigh, he reluctantly called room service.

He was in the middle of eating me out when the knock at the door came. Blondie acted like he wasn't going to budge, so I had to literally push him off me to answer it. I was famished and wasn't going to continue anything until my stomach was happy.

After devouring the fries like I hadn't eaten in days, I just wanted to pass out. He, however, had other ideas. We skipped the warm-up part and went straight into sex. His penis was nicely sized and felt good when he gave it to me. As soon as I got comfortable he shot his load and went down to eat me out. All in a matter of ninety seconds. I didn't come here for oral. I wanted dick. When I mentioned it to him he said he wouldn't be able to get it up because he was too drunk. I immediately moved to the other bed and went to sleep. I was over it.

I hopped in my Uber around 7 a.m., hair a disaster and makeup smudged across my face. I couldn't help but burst out laughing when the driver asked if I was headed to work. "No girl, this is my drive home of shame."

You probably shouldn't sleep with someone if you need alcohol to do so. Advice from an unsatisfied woman.

Mac Daddy and Bombshell

I was twenty-eight and fully immersed in an older man fetish. These feelings had been building since my sexcapade with Bar Master. There was just something about being with someone double my age and experience that really revved my engine. Plus, it didn't hurt that the bulk of my income came from the older category. Men were automatically more attractive when they gave me money.

I was ready to head home after the best night of my stripping career. What I used to make in one month was bursting out of my wallet from the previous six hours of work. I was practically skipping to the dressing room when a host flagged me down, telling me that a big spender had just arrived and that I was definitely his type. Even though it was 4 a.m., I turned around and made my way to him. I used to pray for this kind of money, so I wasn't about to pass up the chance to make more just because I was a little tired.

Mac Daddy sat there like the king of the castle, dressed in expensive clothes and wearing a watch worth more than some people's annual salary. Despite his intimidating presence, I approached him with confidence. Nothing was going to bring me down from the high of my night.

I sat down beside him and greeted him with a warm hello, but he responded with nothing but silence and a cold, icy stare. His gray-blue eyes tried to cut through me as I held his gaze. Just looking at him started to irritate me, so after a ten-second standoff, I stood up to leave. But before I could, he grabbed my forearm, pulled me onto his lap, wrapped his arms around me, and whispered a soft "hi" in my ear. A shiver ran down my spine. I wasn't sure whether to be annoyed by his silence or turned on by the way I felt in his arms. "He talks," I said, unable to hide the mix of surprise and intrigue in my voice.

He poured me a glass of champagne and told me to "stay" as he gestured for another dancer to join us. Thank goodness I didn't have to deal with him alone. Everything he said only reinforced that he was a self-absorbed, high-horse rider—the kind of customer I despised. To make any money off these losers, I had to pretend to care about every word that came out of their stupid mouths. My supply of fake enthusiasm was limited. Thankfully all three of us ended up in the VIP room ten painstaking minutes later.

After the host took our payment, I positioned myself in front of him to start dancing. But just as I was about to sit on his lap, this motherfucker slapped my ass harder than

I've ever been slapped in my life. Infuriated, I spun around with my fist pulled back, ready to knock him the fuck out. The other dancer saw my anger and quickly stepped in, putting a hand on me to calm me down while scolding him for such a senseless move. He just sat there, grinning like he was proud of himself for getting a reaction out of me. I had to dig deep to find any ounce of calm to keep myself from going bat shit crazy on this fucker. How dare he put his hands on me like that.

Since I'd already been paid, I spent the rest of our private hour talking about food, looking for a menu, ordering food, eating food, and then breathing my French fry-scented breath as close to his face as possible—while keeping my conversation to an absolute minimum for this shit bag. When our time was finally up, I looked him straight in the eye and told him I hoped he got stuck behind a slow-moving Toyota every time he was in a hurry. I wasn't even trying to be funny. I genuinely hated him.

I managed to push the whole incident out of my mind—until a week later when I spotted him back at the club, standing right next to Captain Try Too Hard. Of course, these two idiots would be friends. I rolled my eyes and tried to slip by unnoticed. But Mac Daddy caught sight of me, abruptly stopped his conversation, latched onto my arm, and led me straight to the VIP room

I seriously considered making a run for it, but the broke girl I used to be scolded me for even thinking about walking away from the money I was about to make. Screw it, I told myself—it was going to be just like last time: the least amount of effort for the most amount of cash.

As our time together began, I pulled out every conversation prompt I knew to make it seem like I really cared about getting to know him. He ate it all up, responding with enthusiasm and playful banter. The hour flew by without any dancing involved. I was surprised when he agreed to do another one.

Our conversation got deeper over the next hour as I straddled him with my bra intact and his hands gently caressing my back. Every stripper dreams of pay-to-talk customers that don't want a dance. This was the easiest VIP I had ever done. I never expected a night like this to come from someone I'd completely despised a week ago.

To keep him on his toes, I played hard to get, pretending he had to convince me to give him my number. But as soon as he pulled me close and whispered that he couldn't wait to feel all of me, I was done for. I couldn't hide my desire as I melted into his arms.

We exchanged texts for a couple of days before agreeing to meet at the bar next to his high-rise condo. I wasn't ready to sleep with him just yet, but I was definitely intrigued by his insistence on introducing me to his stripper girlfriend—who supposedly loved girls.

We were working on our second bottle of champagne when his stunning twenty-two-year-old blonde bombshell of a girlfriend arrived. Everyone's head turned as soon as she walked in. Her slender yet curvy figure was a masterpiece of feminine perfection. Each sway of her shoulder-length hair seemed to frame her flawless face and beautiful features with effortless grace. Her form-fitting outfit only enhanced her magnetic presence. She could leave both men and women speechless in her wake. I was completely captivated as she introduced herself with a warm hug.

We spent the next few hours laughing and getting to know each other. Not only was she gorgeous but she was intelligent and funny. We quickly discovered we both shared a love for nicotine, so we snuck off to the restroom together to indulge—Mac Daddy wasn't a fan of his women smoking

We giggled at our predicament in the confined space of the stall as we passed the cigarette back and forth. All I could think about was closing the gap between us, and I could feel she wanted the same. As if synchronized, we both leaned in, eager to taste each other. Her touch was tender and her lips soft and delicate against mine. I gently cradled the back of her neck as our tongues danced perfectly together. Every part of her drew me in. She pulled back and invited me to join her and Mac Daddy that night and I couldn't say yes fast enough.

We returned to the bar hand in hand, feeling more intoxicated than when we left. As soon as we reached Mac Daddy I placed my hands on her hips and pulled her close while pressing her back against the bar. I planted another kiss on her perfectly shaped lips and basked in the feeling of everyone in the bar lusting after us. I wanted to taste all of her.

We walked across the street to Mac Daddy's penthouse where a spread of champagne, strawberries, and whipped cream awaited us. We poured a round of drinks and danced around his luxurious place as our clothes flew off. Before I knew it, I found myself lying on the kitchen island, with Bombshell girl on top of me. Her perfect everything tangled up in my embrace. She skillfully slid down my body with her hard nipples grazing me along the way. She was so sexy. Nothing else in the room mattered. Especially Mac Daddy watching from the side.

A tickle of excitement coursed through my body as she reached my clit with her mouth. Her cool lips worked their way around with skill. This was *by far* the hottest thing I had ever experienced in my whole entire life. I had never been so turned on.

We headed to the bedroom to keep the momentum going, but at this point, Mac Daddy was just starting to annoy me. He barely did anything except stand there in the corner, looking like a creep. And when he finally decided to join in, he ended up spraying whipped cream all over my lady parts. We had to pause everything for a solid ten minutes to explain why whipped cream in that area caused unwanted things. You'd think a sexually active fifty-five-year-old man with two ex-wives would know something this basic. Total buzzkill.

Me and Bombshell moved back to the bed after we cleaned off the sticky mess. Wack Daddy stood on the side trying to figure out what to do with himself. I silently willed him to leave. I didn't want any distractions from the matter at hand. I had never eaten a woman out before and I was slightly nervous. I knew what felt good to me and watched enough porn to see what felt good to others but actually doing it was a whole different ball game. I positioned myself on top of her so I could kiss her juicy lips again. I slowly moved down to her perfect little nipples, tasting her as much as possible along the way. I couldn't get over how smooth she was. I continued downward until I reached my destination. I reminded myself not to rush as I kissed around and breathed in her scent. She sexily instructed me to "lick my clit." Well okay, I guess we'll get right to the point. I had a mini panic attack as my brain yelled at me to "Find the clit! Find the clit." I guess she was over this foreplay nonsense.

I moved my inexperienced tongue over her smooth sweet spot and used every move I could remember from the last lesbian sex scene I saw. Full tongue, circle tongue, slow tongue, up and down tongue. She liked the last one best. I was affirmed in my efforts by the sounds she was making. When I scooped both my hands under her perfect ass, I felt her back arch and legs tense. I held her pulsating body close so I could finish her off. Her high-pitched moan told me I succeeded, while validating my whole existence. I thought a woman eating me out was the hottest thing but making a woman come was even hotter. Wack Daddy had left the room at some point when he realized that no one wanted him there. Thank goodness.

As I made my exit, I could hear Bombshell and Wack Daddy arguing. He wasn't her boyfriend; he was actually her sugar daddy—and he was upset that no one was giving him attention. I couldn't help but smile to myself. That was the price he paid for slapping my ass so hard when we first met.

I couldn't see myself being with a woman full-time, but I was definitely open to another night of it—preferably without a man lurking in the corner.

Karma has no menu.
You get served what you deserve.

Bullet Bill

It was the summer of 2017, and I found myself in Nashville to witness the solar eclipse. My friends had planned a two-day getaway and convinced me to join them at the last minute—and I was so glad they did. We danced on a rooftop, champagne flowing freely, as we gazed up at the sky through our eclipse-viewing glasses. This was the life.

I was having such a good time that, when my friends left, I decided to extend my stay for another night. I had come to cherish solo moments of exploration and there was something about the city that called to me.

I started my day by wandering through museums, soaking in the culture, then lucked into last-minute tickets to an unforgettable concert at the legendary Grand Ole Opry. Afterward, I indulged in a hearty Southern dinner at Acme Feed & Seed, before answering the call of the honky-tonks that lined Broadway. The energy of the streets was electric, and I found myself swept into the vibrant, lively atmosphere.

I spun around on the crowded dance floor with a cold beer as my only companion. I felt liberated. I didn't have any desire to make new friends as I reveled in the joy of simply existing. It wasn't until well past midnight when I decided to call it a night.

I sat at a bus stop at the end of the street, weighing my options: save a few bucks and walk the twenty-five minutes back to my hotel on a quiet, dimly lit road, or splurge on an overpriced Uber that would take twenty minutes to arrive. After a brief pause, I chose caution over cost and made myself comfortable for the wait.

Everything was eerily silent as my senses acclimated to the stillness of the night. A sense of peaceful euphoria washed over me, until the tranquility was shattered by the sound of heavy footsteps approaching. I knew it had to be a man making this much of a commotion. Rather than fear, a rush of excitement surged through me as I turned to see who was coming. I laid my eyes on a striking figure who was wearing cowboy boots that seemed to echo against the pavement. We met each other's gaze, and in that instant, my mind raced with a dozen wild possibilities.

He flashed a charming smile and greeted me with a warm, "Hello, beautiful," before casually taking the empty seat next to me on the bench. "We should be friends," he said with a confident grin. I agreed, and without thinking twice, I canceled my ride so we could talk.

At first, the conversation was engaging—there was an ease to it. But as the minutes passed, my interest started to wane. Every time I asked one of those typical "getting to know you" questions, his answers seemed to circle back to his job and his intense obsession with guns. It felt like we were stuck in a loop, and I found myself losing interest.

By 2 a.m., the exhaustion from the day's excitement was taking its toll. Bullet Bill suggested I join him at his place, about forty-five minutes away. That was a definite no. I wasn't about to venture off into the unknown with a complete stranger. But despite my hesitation, I still found him attractive enough to have some fun. So, I decided to flip the script and invited him to my hotel instead.

He walked over to the passenger side of his truck, parked just behind us, and gallantly opened the door for me. I loved the chivalry. We listened to country music and sang together on our brief five-minute drive. I was thrilled for what was to come.

I jumped out of the truck as soon as we arrived, only to realize he wasn't following me. When I turned around, I was met with the sight of Bullet Bill completely absorbed in loading and unloading a 9mm Glock. *What the fuck?* I was in no mood for this nonsense. If I hadn't just endured a two-hour monologue about his obsession with guns, I might've had a heart attack. But instead, all I felt was irritation. I was ready for some bedtime dick—not a gun lesson. I had to sit there for what felt like an eternity, while he insisted on showing me "gun techniques." Normally, my sapiosexual side might've appreciated this kind of intellectual diversion, but not at the hour of "fuck me o'clock."

After telling him I wasn't going to spend my whole night in a truck, I finally got him to step out, but he insisted on bringing his gun along. When I asked why, he shrugged and said, "I've seen war zones. I'm not about to die in a hotel room." I couldn't help but laugh at the idea of little ol' me taking down this massive 6'4" guy. While I knew I wasn't a psycho, I could understand his hesitation. After all, we had just met at a deserted bus stop in the dead of night—a situation that screamed "stranger danger." In hindsight, I probably should've been the one armed.

After a quick shower and downstairs landscape, I joined him on the bed. Fresh and ready. He kissed me gently as I slid perfectly into his embrace. That's when it went from zero to really freaking cringy. He proceeded to go through five-second spurts of aggressive intensity where he mauled my face with his lips while dry humping me like a tweaker virgin. I had to tell him to simmer the fuck down. Which he did, until thirty seconds later when he spazzed out again. To make everything even more cringy, he asked me if he could practice eating me out because he had never done it before. I was about to lose it. It was 3:30 in the damn morning and I didn't sign up to give a sex ed lesson to a forty-year-old man. I wanted to fuck.

I reluctantly let him go down on me, only because I needed a break from the spaz attacks. Boy, was that a mistake. This grown man plopped his bristly face on my delicate lady parts and scraped it from left to right until I almost kicked him back to the bench we'd met on. He didn't even open his mouth! It was absolutely horrible. I told him with obvious distaste that we needed to move on from this. Ouch.

He then started pestering me to suck his dick. I swear he was on another planet. I had the common courtesy of showering when we got to my room; he did not. I wasn't about to taste a penis that had been marinating in the Nashville heat all night. Fuck that.

I ignored everything he was saying as I went to my bag to get a condom. Bullet Bill then tried to persuade me to have sex without one. This guy was clearly not right in the head. I had no idea who he actually was or where his penis had been. The last thing I wanted was an STD or an oopsie baby. I firmly told him to shut up and put it on. He reluctantly complied, his lips curling into a boyish pout.

All my annoyance slipped away when he slowly eased his good-sized member inside of me. Yay, sex! It had been about three months since the last time, and I was more than ready for it. I was just starting to forget about the previous hour when it happened again. That five-second seizure of roughness. This time including violent penis thrusts. This guy had no idea what he was doing. What a disaster. I had to make it end but I still wanted an orgasm. I let out the sexiest moan I could muster in an attempt to make him think that he was doing a really good job. All while I touched myself vigorously. Normally that got guys off. Not this one. I managed a weak finish just in time for him to be overcome with whiskey dick. Huge shout-out to the cosmic forces for that ending. I couldn't tolerate another minute of him.

I showered once more and climbed back into bed, eager for some sleep. I watched Bullet Bill meticulously ensure that his gun was loaded before placing it on the nightstand beside him. All I could think was "'Merica." I was too tired and annoyed to be scared for my life. So I switched off the lights and breathed a sigh of relief as I welcomed in a dimension that was better than the current one. I was almost on my first dream when I felt this man-child try to mount me. I pretended to sleep. I would have rather eaten dirt than have any more interactions with him. It took him ten minutes to take the hint. He grunted defeatedly as he rolled over. An hour later he did the same fucking thing. Waking me out of a dead sleep like a needy child. I scolded him and told him that it was time to leave. The sun was peeking through the blinds at this point and I had a day to get started. He was one of the most irritating people I have ever met.

We exchanged numbers, but I blocked him as soon as his truck drove out of the parking lot. What a ridiculous night.

Every person you meet has a story, but not every story is one you should be a part of.

Bootyhole Bandit

It was a random Wednesday in Vegas, and my girlfriend and I decided to hit the town. I'd been working non-stop, barely taking advantage of living in the party capital of the world. It was time to let loose and have some fun.

Despite spending extra time on my hair, makeup, and lady landscape, my main goal was to have a carefree, wild night with my friend. Looking my best always made me feel my best. I slipped into my most flattering dress, stepped out the door, and strutted down the hall like the sexy, powerful enchantress I was.

The upscale venue was packed when we arrived, and while I wasn't looking for romance, I couldn't help but notice the impressive lineup of men. I tried my best to ignore them, settling at the bar with my friend for a drink, but nearly fell off my seat when I glanced to my right. Leaning against a table, just within arm's reach, was the hottest guy I'd seen in ages. My "no-dick" mantra instantly flew out the window. I watched him sip his beer, casually surveying the room, completely unaware of my thoughts—until he caught me staring. I couldn't resist saying hello.

After some casual small talk, I suggested we move to a quieter couch, away from the crowd clamoring for the bartender's attention. As we sat down, I subtly brushed my leg against his, inching it closer with each drink. When my friend went to the bathroom, it was clear we were both feeling the chemistry and a kiss was imminent. Just as I was about to lean in, a sudden thought made me pause. I asked him, point-blank, if he was married. His eyes told me everything before he even opened his mouth.

My friend returned as I was angrily demanding why he wasn't wearing a wedding ring. His lame attempt at justifying it made my blood boil. I excused myself to the restroom, before I chose violence.

I shouldn't have been surprised. It was Vegas, after all, where most married men step off the plane with their wedding rings tucked in their pockets. I just assumed it was only the ones heading to the strip clubs. Turns out, I was wrong.

When I returned, my friend was still sitting with him, so I had no choice but to join them—I wasn't about to stand at the bar alone. He immediately started apologizing, insisting he never meant to lead me on, that he loved his wife deeply and would "never" cheat on her.

Bullshit.

He knew exactly what he was doing and was now trying to cover it up. I decided that I was going to teach him a lesson. I would seduce him all night and then ghost him at the end. That's what he deserved for being a shitty husband.

After he finished his stupid apology I looked him dead in the face and said, "I'm going to fuck you tonight and you're going to like it." His eyes smoldered as the words sank in. He liked that. Dirty fuck.

I really did want to ditch him with a hard-on, but as the night and double vodkas flowed my resolve began to slip. I craved the forbidden despite swearing I wouldn't. Part of me wanted to leave, but more of me wanted to stay. Alcohol is a hell of a drug.

In a sexual trance I grazed my hand over his dick as I lay it to rest on his inner thigh. I bit my lip between words of lust while looking at him alluringly. He had wanted me from the moment he laid eyes on me, and I knew it. My inner seductress took control and I demanded that he kiss me. He leaned in without hesitation.

I was bent over the side of his bed in no time. He hastily pulled up my dress and yanked off my thong so he could bury his face in my lower lips. I welcomed his warm tongue with legs wide open. I was about to turn around and return the favor when he slid up to lick between my butt cheeks. Dirty boy. He slowly eased his tongue into my bootyhole until it couldn't go any further. Then he proceeded to fuck me with it as I placed the mini vibrator I grabbed from the hotel's pleasure pack on my clit. I came in no time. I turned around to grab his fat dick and sucked it roughly until it was throbbing hard. He liked when it hit the back of my throat so I let him face fuck me until his manly moan gave me the signal I needed to climb on top and ride him like a bull until we both finished together. Talk about pent-up tension. Our drunk selves rolled over and fell asleep immediately. This was some good sex.

The sun woke me up a couple hours later. I looked over to see this man still sporting the condom. Gross. I felt bad for his wife. She had no idea that she was married to a pig. I hoped that karma wasn't going to get me back for this one. Was I even in the wrong? I wasn't the one who made any vows to anyone. Oh well.

I crept out of the bed and back into my clothes from the evening. I then quietly slipped out the door without him opening his eyes. Escape success. Adios Bootyhole Bandit.

Sleeping with a married person gives you a moment of attention with no benefit to your future.

Euro Lover

Oh, Euro Lover. The thought of him pounding me makes my insides throb.

Two years had flown by since I started stripping. I never imagined I'd last this long, nor did I think I could actually make a living from dancing and partying with people. But then again, that's Vegas—anything goes here.

It was 7 a.m., and I was still at work. The past few nights hadn't been as profitable as I'd hoped, so I decided to stay late to make up for it. Tired but determined, I scanned the crowd for any potential bank account benefactors. That's when I spotted him—dancing like he owned the place.

Normally, I thought men who danced at strip clubs were big losers. But he was attractive and looked like he had money, and the pickings were slim.

I startled him out of his dance trance by placing myself abruptly in front of him to say hello. I loved the surprise-attack icebreaker. I watched his shock turn into desire as I looked deeply into his dark brown eyes. He took a moment to stare back at me before introducing himself in a deep European accent that sent warm tremors down my spine.

After a quick get to know each other chat, I discovered that he was one of those "never pay for dances" types. It came as no surprise; he fit the profile. Even though I was exhausted, challenge accepted. I gently guided him to a seat so I could sit on his lap. It was seduction time. But before I could get a word in, he started rambling about his career as a porn star and how tough it was. Definitely didn't see this on the bingo card for the night. I nodded along and pretended to be interested as I formulated a plan to get him into my bed. I never thought a porn star would make it onto my bucket list, but there I was imagining how good the sex would be with someone with that much experience.

I took a steadying breath when he told me how much he despised meaningless sex and just wanted to make love. "Me freaking too," I yelled on the inside, all while keeping my composure. I didn't want to come off as too eager. Instead, I let him keep talking, my fingers gently tracing the back of his neck as I listened.

He tipped me for hanging out, and we exchanged numbers. In the middle of it all, he bluntly said that if we ended up having sex, he wanted it to be nice and soft.

Followed by "I don't want to fuck you hard…. Unless you want me too. Then I will." I almost had to pick my jaw off of the floor. Hell yes I wanted him to fuck me hard. His subtle confidence left me at a loss for words. I was ravenous for him.

We set up a coffee date for the next day. I arrived early, slipping into a corner seat, hoping he'd look as good in the daylight as he did in the dim light of the club. My nerves were starting to get the best of me until a tall, handsome man in a perfectly tailored suit walked in. My heart skipped a beat.

I couldn't help but devour him with my eyes as he made his way over to me. He seemed a little nervous, so I held back the advances I was dying to make. His accent was so much more noticeable now than it had been the night before. Our conversation kept hitting pauses as we relied on Google Translate to bridge the gaps in understanding. I laughed when he told me that alcohol gave him English speaking superpowers. It seemed so.

We agreed to take the party across the street to my place. As we walked, I asked how long he'd been in the industry, and he casually dropped that he wasn't really a porn star—it was just drunk talk. I wasn't sure whether to believe him. The pretend "crisis" he'd shared seemed a little too real to be made up. Although I was disappointed that my new fantasy of being with a porn star wasn't going to happen, I was still determined to have a sexy time with him.

I poured him a glass of white wine as soon as we got to my place. It had been sitting on my counter for months, and I figured it was the perfect time to finally crack it open. *Wrong.* I'd forgotten that wine was a big deal in his culture, so offering him cheap, room-temperature white wine was probably the least hospitable thing I could've done. He took a sip, scrunched up his face, and immediately handed the glass back to me, clearly offended. I couldn't stop laughing—at both him and myself. He didn't get why I found it so funny, which only made it funnier.

I looked into his eyes after finishing my laughing fit and he leaned down to kiss me. Our tongues twirled perfectly together as our passion for the moment grew. We moved to my room where he continued to enjoy my body with his sensual mouth. His experienced hands moved to all the places that made my insides happy. He was at my clit in no time. Making sure to kiss around before giving me the gratification I was arching for. His juicy lips surrounded my flower as his sweet tongue swirled in all the right ways. He moved back up to my neck while making sure I could feel his big, hard cock pressing against me. He slowly caressed me as he slid in the tip just enough for me to use my body to beg for more. I grabbed his arms and wrapped my legs around him tightly until he finally filled me up with his manhood. He slowly thrusted in a way that wasn't too rough but just enough for me to know who was in charge. I started to feel the tickle inside that signaled the orgasm I craved. It was building up stronger and stronger until I could no longer hold back. I finished loudly as I felt him grow two more inches inside of me. I couldn't believe there was more. He prolonged my ecstasy by giving it to me firmly until he finished with a deep, satisfying grunt.

We basked in the moment together as he gently lay on top of me. It felt so right. It was an immediate yes when he asked me not to go to work. Neither of us wanted our time with each other to end. He slid his hand passionately down to my satisfied lady parts and commented on how warm they were. I told him that I was still turned on. I didn't realize how much of a language barrier there really was until I had to spend ten minutes trying to explain what "turned on" meant. We laughed simultaneously when he finally understood. Then without another word he turned me over and gave it to me like every woman secretly wants it. Sticking it to me so hard that my whole body shook with delight. I had never been fucked so good.

Maybe he really was a porn star.

As we lay there, catching our breath for the second time, he casually dropped that he was married with two kids. What. The. Actual. Fuck. I had no words. Then, as if that wasn't enough, he asked if I'd consider moving to Europe to be with him. I fought hard to keep from laughing and responded, "Hell fucking no." He went quiet, and I watched as deep emotions flickered across his face. Out of nowhere, a tear rolled down his cheek. Um…what? He had a whole damn family back home! What is wrong with these men?

After a short cuddle his phone started ringing. I left the room to shower so he could talk with his wife. What a trip.

When I made my way back to the bed, he kept pestering me to dance for him. It was annoying—honestly, the last thing I wanted to do when I wasn't working was put on a show for someone. But since he'd given me a couple of the best orgasms of my life, I caved.

I put my lap dance playlist on along with my sexiest stripper outfit and stepped toward him. His eyes simmered with longing. It was as if it was his first time seeing me. I grazed his cock as I ran my fingers from his inner thighs all the way to his nipples. I placed my lips softly on his neck while slowly mounting him. I circled my hips as I pressed my lady parts against his awakening pleasure stick. When the next song started, I kept my body in motion as I unclasped my bra and placed my breasts in his face. He breathed in deeply as he let the scent of my freshly showered body fill him. I kissed his neck all the way down to his chest. Circling his nipples with my tongue as I continued my path down to his hard penis. I slowly licked his balls while I lightly grasped his shaft. Stroking it as I continued my seduction. I traced my tongue all the way up to the tip where I alternated between my lips. I wrapped him inside of my mouth while circling my tongue all the way around, pushing him deeper until he moaned. Feeling him fully harden in my mouth was so hot. He gently placed his hands on my face and brought me up to his. He didn't come but it seemed as if I had just fulfilled some sort of fantasy by the way he couldn't stop kissing me.

We stayed in this bubble of love for what seemed like forever. No orgasm. No sex. Just cuddles and kisses. I never wanted to leave but I was starving. I decided that pizza was the way to go. I rolled onto my stomach so I could grab my phone from the nightstand. As I was placing the order I felt his hands creep to my hips. By the time I picked out the toppings his tongue was lathering all my sexual places from behind. Before I could hang up the phone my legs were spread apart and his perfect penis was thrusting inside of me. I screamed out in pleasure as I quickly ended the conversation. He gently pushed me flat onto my stomach with one hand while he lifted my leg to the side with the other. I felt him go deeper. I turned my head so I could watch him take me how he wanted. His manly sighs filled me with such gratification that I didn't even mind that I didn't come. We lay together in complete bliss for the third time that night.

By the time the pizza arrived, I was starving. I set it down on the table and was about to dive in when Euro Lover asked for a plate and utensils. I'd forgotten his native country's customs again. I watched, amused, as he neatly sliced and ate his pizza with the precision of someone at a five-star restaurant, while I tore into mine with my hands and chomped it down like a savage. He laughed and said I ate like his six-year-old. I grinned and kept going—classy as always.

He glanced at the time with a look of sadness, realizing his flight was in a couple of hours. He had to leave. I walked him to the entrance of my condo, where a cab was waiting. He looked me in the eye with tears brimming and told me he loved me in his language. I said it back and he left, never to be seen again.

> *Your soul mate is not another person's husband.*

New York

In the summer of my twenty-ninth year, I planned a trip to Manhattan with Bar Master so that I could experience a sex club. Despite working in the industry, I'd never actually stepped foot in a place specifically made for fucking. Bar Master had been a few times, so I trusted him to show me the ropes—literally.

We started the evening with dinner and hookah before heading to our destination. He looked handsome in suit pants and a button-down shirt, while I wore a tight red dress without any undergarments for easy access. In the middle of dinner, he asked what I was hoping to get out of the night. I appreciated how easy it was to talk openly with him. I shared my fantasy of a having an orgy, and he responded with reassurance, telling me he was open to whatever I wanted since it was my first time, not his. Such a gentleman. After wrapping up our meal with a couple of vodka shots, we made our way to the club.

As soon as we arrived, I realized I was far too sober for this. I hadn't expected a five-star venue, but I definitely wasn't prepared for how miserable it felt. The staff looked like they hated their lives, and the guests—well, they looked like they'd just stumbled in off the street. Despite my disappointment, I'd come too far to turn back now. The only solution was alcohol. So, we checked in our things and made our way to the bar on the second floor.

After a few more shots, I felt settled enough to focus on my surroundings rather than just the people. The room was long and narrow, with erotic furniture lining the walls. The dim lighting made it feel comfortable to be naked. The smell of cleaning solution in the air was also a reassuring touch. A woman was tied to an X-frame while being pleasured loudly by her partner's fingers. Clearly relishing in all the room's attention being directed to her. I too enjoyed the scene while admiring her boldness and vulnerability.

I was almost at the alcohol level I needed to be in order to enjoy this grungy place, so we stepped outside for a quick smoke. On our way back, we had to climb over a different couple who had decided that the narrow stairway would be a perfect place to give each other oral. It was refreshing to see people without inhibitions.

We ordered another drink as we debated whether we were ready for the third floor. The screaming woman and her partner had left, but the three couples who had been watching them remained, likely deciding their next move as well. I took one last look at the sexless dungeon and decided to head up.

As our feet hit the stairs, I glanced behind to see the voyeurs trailing closely at our heels. They were clearly hoping for another show, probably eager for Bar Master and me to put on a performance. We were, without a doubt, the most attractive people there.

We sat near the entrance, still curious about the experience; I wasn't quite ready to dive into sex. Our followers trickled in behind us, thankfully scattering into the room's dimly lit corners. Two of the eight king-sized mattresses on the floor were already in use: one by a shy couple in the corner, tenderly making love, and another by the couple with the loud lady, who was now causing quite a commotion. As she was being rammed, I noticed the wet spot on the mattress growing larger in tandem with her escalating screams. I watched in awe, as despite all my sexual experience, I had never managed to squirt. I wondered if I ever would.

As we continued to watch, a couple we hadn't noticed before entered the room and introduced themselves. I was immediately drawn to the man, though not the woman. They were from a conservative country where sex and its exploration were heavily taboo, and they'd come to New York specifically to experience this kind of freedom. They were pleasant to talk to, but I had to politely decline their offer to join them in a private room—I wasn't comfortable being in a situation where I'd have to be intimate with the wife. I finished the last of my drink, watching them leave the room. Even though we didn't have anyone to play with, I was finally drunk enough for some fun with my friend and his well-endowed member.

I sat on his lap and rested my hand on his inner thigh

to signal that I was ready. As our lips connected, all I could taste was the ashy remnants of the hookah from dinner. I tried to ignore it but then he started doing this weird thing with his tongue by shoving it deeply into my mouth and curling it upward to boop my palate with the tip. I absolutely hated it. I was trying to have a sensual make-out session and he was trying to show off how long his tongue was. It was so dumb. I suggested we have sex so I could avoid anything to do with his mouth.

We moved to the divider between the seating area and the mattresses. He lifted up my dress as he bent me over it. I watched the whole room watch us. I could now understand why the screaming girl liked it so much. There was something about performing for an audience that turned me on even more. I could feel the warmth build as he slowly eased himself in.

As he picked up the pace, a cute couple emerged from the shadows and began having fun on a nearby mattress. I felt a silent connection with the woman as we observed each other getting it from our men. She was adorable. I watched them pause to exchange a few words before making their way toward us with clear intention.

I replied with an immediate "yes" when she asked if they could join. She leaned over the other side of the divider to take it the same way I was. I put my hand on top of hers as we held the sides of our faces together. She felt lovely. Her lips brushed my ear as she whispered that she wanted to kiss me. I turned my head to meet her. She tasted sweet and moved her tongue gingerly. Our men let us enjoy each other as they continued giving it to us. After a while, her partner asked if we'd be open to switching. I agreed before consulting with mine. His large size was starting to become uncomfortable, and I craved a change.

We moved to one of the empty mattresses. The woman was very petite so I was curious to see if she could handle Bar Master. He laid behind her in the spooning position while I took his penis and guided it toward her. I touched her clit in a circular motion as he pressed himself inside. My new partner was behind me and slowly navigating around my body with his mouth. This was nice. I replaced my fingers with my tongue and felt her take in the nine inches I previously had. She received it like a champ. My new partner placed his hands on my hips and rocked me back onto his perfectly sized cock. I released my lips and arched in the pleasure of this new sensation. It was such a reprieve from Bar Master's anaconda.

I felt sexual chemistry with this mystery man so I was happy when he rolled me on my back to kiss me. He tasted like peppermint and his tongue matched the flow of mine. We let our partners enjoy each other while we created our own world of fun. He fisted my hair as he gave me his nice dick. He was passionate and conscious of every movement I liked. He felt so good. We changed positions again so that I could be on top. It was all going great until I realized the condom broke. Terrified, we exchanged a frantic glance as we processed the situation. I quickly calculated that it was not a big issue because he didn't finish. So we grabbed another condom and carried on. I continued riding him until I knew he was close. I touched myself vigorously until our bodies sighed together loudly in release. Sharing an orgasm is always more satisfying than having one alone.

Everything unfolded so quickly that I forgot there were other people on the bed until I glanced over and saw them watching us. I couldn't help but wonder if I'd put on a good show.

We all shared a hug, exchanged numbers, and then made our way back into the real world—where people don't have public sex. Orgy fantasy: fulfilled!

Two days later, I got a message from the mystery man asking if I had any STDs or was on birth control. Given that we met in the dingy attic of a sex club, it was a fair question. I reassured him that I was clean, though I wasn't using any contraception. He then offered to send me Plan B from Amazon, just in case. I laughed and told him I would absolutely not be taking any mail-order pills, but promised I'd let him know when my next period rolled around. An orgy baby would certainly make for an interesting conversation at Christmas.

*Desire is not something to hide—
it's something to embrace.*

Dud

Dud was a friend of my best friend's husband. Though he was undeniably attractive, his clear indifference toward me made me indifferent to his existence. Our interactions were few, limited to brief hellos exchanged in passing. But everything shifted one New Year's Eve when I returned home for the holidays.

I was at my best friend's house, surrounded by about twenty people, all of us thoroughly hammered. Dud had been hovering around me all night, and I assumed it was just to mess with his friend—who was openly interested in me—to get a rise out of him. Dud was known to do stupid attention-seeking things like that. By the end of the night, I was too drunk to think straight and passed out—curled up in his arms, naturally, since he hadn't left my side for more than a few minutes. As the laughter and chatter of the others faded around me, I drifted into a deep sleep. I couldn't party like I used to.

I woke up as the last person left the room—though it's possible he was the one who woke me, I'm not sure. But lying in his arms felt unexpectedly…right. We both turned toward each other at the same time, and before I knew it, we were making out. The warmth of his affection and the intoxicating feel of his yummy mouth had me spinning. He pulled me on top of him, and the air around us thickened. In the midst of our kissing, I gave him a playful slap on the face, and he smirked, asking if that was all I had. Always up for a challenge, I pulled my hand back and slapped him into speechlessness. I almost cried laughing at his expression. What did he expect? He knew I had a "don't give a shit" attitude. His features softened as the realization of his enjoyment washed over him. Good boy.

As much as I craved more of him, it was late, and the prospect of turning my friend's couch into a trampoline was not on my pre-sleep game plan. I murmured that I was tired and nestled back onto his chest to visit dreamland.

It felt like only five minutes had passed before the blazing rays of the sun jolted me awake. I was drenched in sweat and miserably uncomfortable—couch sleeping was the worst. As I tried to piece together the events of the night through my foggy, hungover brain, my eyes wandered downward and landed on him—completely naked. I guess he was hot too. I took a quick moment to appreciate the view before waking him up so he could get dressed. Who strips down in their friend's living room and then just crashes? Weirdo.

I couldn't stand the thought of another minute on that couch, so I decided to head home to the comfort of my own bed. As I hugged him goodbye, he whispered softly that he wanted to see me again. The words sent a warm rush through me—I felt the same.

For the next two days, every time my phone chimed with a new text, I rushed to check it, hoping it was from him—only to be let down. I didn't understand. He had said he wanted to see me, yet there was no effort on his part to follow through. Was I imagining a connection that wasn't really there? Despite the uncertainty, I couldn't shake the feeling of his kiss. So, I took initiative and suggested we grab drinks. To my relief, he agreed.

As we made plans for the evening, Dud casually mentioned that his friends were heading to a bar and suggested we tag along. I couldn't help but feel a little foolish—I'd thought he was genuinely interested in me. Still, I reluctantly agreed, secretly hoping I could find a way to subtly seduce him throughout the night. Red flags danced synchronously through my mind as I got ready, but I pushed them to the side.

We met at the train station to head downtown together, and I noticed he seemed a bit nervous. Although his lack of confidence wasn't exactly a turn-on, maybe it was a sign he actually liked me and was just a little shy.

That thought vanished the moment we arrived at the bar. He rushed ahead, completely ignoring the simple courtesy of holding the door for me, as though reuniting with his friends was the greatest moment of his life. Never mind that he'd seen them just the day before. It was so rude!

I kept up the pretense as we walked up to their table. His friends were cool, but I wasn't in the mood to socialize—I just wanted to drink and, frankly, get laid. When the server came by, Dud announced loudly that he'd cover the first round, and I could handle the second. What was wrong with this guy? The unspoken rule when you're out with friends is to take turns buying rounds. He didn't need to say it out loud—especially after making it clear that this wasn't a date. But now that he'd insisted I buy him one, I was definitely not going to. I almost walked out, but then I remembered it had been nine months since I'd last saw a penis and I was determined to have his tonight.

The night dragged on as I forced myself to feign interest in their dumb conversation. I wanted to dance, to feel alive, to be somewhere with energy. I knew there was a bar with live music nearby, so I bided my time, waiting for everyone to loosen up a little before suggesting we go. Dud was the only one who seemed excited about the change of scenery. The rest of his friends declined. I half-heartedly tried to convince them as we made our way toward the exit, but no one budged. My heart skipped a beat—I knew that if I could get him alone, there was a good chance I could get the penis date that I wanted.

Just as we were about to step through the door, Dud grabbed one of his friends and literally dragged him down the street with us. A sinking feeling hit me—he clearly didn't want to be alone with me. It was obvious, but I didn't want to admit it. Still, I decided to stick to my plan of seduction. I was determined to get what I wanted, no matter how he felt. We clearly didn't have anything in common anyway, so there was no point in getting attached.

It was Spanish night at the venue, and my salsa hips were ready to groove. Dud had mentioned he knew how to dance on the way there, so I grabbed his hand and pulled him straight to the floor as soon as we walked in. Turns out, he'd lied. For the next hour, I found myself trying to teach him the moves while his friend awkwardly lingered nearby, unsure what to do with himself.

While we were taking a break, an older gentleman asked me to dance. I left the boys at the bar and joined him on the floor—I was eager to have some real fun. One of the things I love about Spanish clubs is how everyone dances with everyone, no matter who you're with. Grandpa twirled me around with such ease that I lost track of time. His skill was so impressive I had to work to keep up. After a few more dances with others, I rejoined Dud and his friend. They looked bored, their enthusiasm nowhere near mine, but I didn't care.

After a few more drinks, his friend finally decided to leave, giving me the chance to execute my plan. I positioned myself in front of him, letting my hips sway against him as we danced to the band's music. He pulled back almost immediately, but not before I felt his manhood swell. A smile tugged at my lips, but I played it cool, pretending not to notice. I knew I would get what I wanted.

By the time we left, we were pretty hammered, so I

suggested we grab a bite to eat. He still hadn't invited me back to his place, so I was trying to stall without making it too obvious that I was horny. I nestled close to him as we walked to the burrito spot, but my stomach dropped when, just five steps in, he pulled out his phone and called his friend—the one who had just left—to come join us again.

Was he really this clueless? Or was I the one who was dumb for holding onto the words he'd whispered to me after our first kiss? Did he not want to see me again? Did he not want to get laid? Did he have herpes? I was confused. I'd given him the "I want to fuck you" look more than once. Did I really need to brush past his dick another five times to get the message across? How much clearer could I be? The whole situation was excruciating.

We ate with his drunk friend and watched him stumble into his cab as we sat on a bench outside, shivering in the cold. At that moment, I decided I was done playing coy. I didn't care whether he liked me or not—I wanted his dick inside of me. I looked him in the eye and told him straight up, "I'm either calling an Uber home or coming to your place." He looked surprised and asked if I was serious. *How much more fucking serious could I make this?*

After showering separately, we crawled into bed together, picking up where we'd left off the week before. His fresh-smelling skin felt irresistible against mine as I wrapped myself around him. He grabbed my wrist and sensually kissed it before trailing his lips up my arm and down my whole body. He placed his face into the v between my thighs and devoured me with his tongue. He was so good. He then rolled onto his back and instructed me to sit on his face. I held myself above him while grinding my hips on his inviting mouth. I loved it. He loved it. I almost came twice. I returned the favor by spinning around and caressing his solid dick with my lips. I was hot and ready for him. He rolled me onto my back so he could suck on my nipples. Then brought himself up to my face as he slowly eased himself in. We gasped in each other's mouth as I felt every inch of his perfect penis fill me up. We were both hungry for each other. He fucked me between kisses, gentle to start. He placed one of his hands in mine as he lifted it over my head and pumped his hips into me until we came loudly together. I fell asleep in his arms right after. Maybe he did actually like me.

When I opened my eyes again, it was morning, and his bed—and the entire apartment—were empty. I pulled the blankets tighter around me, savoring the warmth, and let myself bask in the lingering sweetness of what felt like the beginning of something new. A love affair I hoped would continue.

I heard the front door open, followed by the sound of bags rustling before it closed. It sounded like he'd gone shopping. He peeked his head into the room to check if I was awake, and I reached out, pulling him into my arms, craving one more cuddle before we started the day. We tangled together, and he whispered that he'd picked up breakfast for us. I thought it was incredibly sweet, especially coming from someone I'd come to realize had no idea how to express their emotions.

My body hummed with satisfaction as he drove me home, each intimate moment replaying in my mind. I couldn't shake the feeling—I had to see him again before I left for Vegas.

The night before my flight, we planned a sleepover. He left his front door unlocked, allowing me to let myself in once I finished all my last-minute travel preparations.

I arrived at his bedroom around 11:30 p.m., and the steady rise and fall of his chest told me he was deeply asleep. I quietly undressed and slipped under the covers beside him. Gently, I traced my fingers along his arm, leaning in to kiss him softly. Slowly, his eyes fluttered open, and he pulled me close, letting me feel that he was happy to see me. We kissed passionately as I took off his boxers and went down on him. He refused to let me pleasure him without reciprocating so he demanded I bring myself around. I placed my wet pussy on his face and couldn't stop myself from coming immediately. We had passionate goodbye sex and dozed off in each other's arms again. I didn't want to leave.

When he left for work at 6 a.m., he told me to sleep as long as I needed. He worked at the airport where my flight was departing later that evening, and he offered to meet me before I left, so I could return his key and he could see me one last time. I couldn't help but smile—I felt the same way.

We both knew the distance might make it hard for us to work long-term, but I couldn't help imagining a more "normal" non-stripper life with him. I wasn't going to push anything, but I decided to leave him a small parting gift—a book we'd talked about. I didn't think it was a huge deal; I just hoped it would remind him of our little piece of time together when he read it. I hadn't done anything romantic for anyone since my last boyfriend, so it felt both vulnerable and exciting.

I held him tightly during our final goodbye at the airport. Though my heart was heavy, I found joy in the anticipation of him discovering my surprise. After kissing him deeply, I mentioned that he would have something special to find when he went home.

When I landed, I eagerly checked my phone, hoping to see a message from him about discovering what I'd left. But there was nothing. Maybe he hadn't been home yet, so I waited. And waited. And waited. After seven days, it finally hit me: he actually didn't give a shit about me.

What I'd left him was a small, thoughtful gesture—nothing grand, but meaningful. Even if he wasn't interested in me, his complete lack of acknowledgment said everything about his character. Over the next year, he would occasionally slide into my messages, never once acknowledging the gift but always insisting we talk. He'd keep me on the phone for hours, making me believe he was invested in some kind of future with me—only to disappear for weeks after what seemed like meaningful conversations. I fell for it a couple of times before finally cutting him off completely. The excitement I'd felt about possibly finding "my person" faded as quickly as it had come, replaced by the painful realization of what I should've known from the beginning—he was just a dud.

> *Stop picking up the breadcrumbs a guy tosses your way and pretending they're a full meal. If he acts like he's not interested, he's not.*

Massage Man

Sin City was supposed to be a quick six-month pit stop on my journey, but five years later, there I was, living my absolute best life. I was still a stripper, and I loved every minute of it. I wasn't broke anymore—my student loans were paid off, I could travel whenever I woke up and felt like it, and I had the freedom to afford whatever my heart desired. I was living the life I'd always dreamed of.

One of my favorite perks of having money was my weekly in-home massage—it was so much more convenient than trekking back and forth to a spa. I had been using the same masseuse for eight months, until he started acting creepy. At first, it was small gifts sporadically, which felt harmless. But then, his touch started getting a little too close to places he shouldn't be near. I knew it was time to find someone new.

I was very selective about whom I trusted with my hard-working body, so I spent a good amount of time researching mobile massage options. Being in Vegas, I knew I'd have to sift through a few weirdos before finding someone legit. I scrolled past a company with a shirtless man as their advertising photo numerous times before my curiosity got the better of me. I figured it was a marketing ploy for business but was surprised to find they had nothing but five-star reviews. I decided to take a leap of faith and booked an appointment for that evening. Even if the guy didn't have washboard abs, I knew I'd still get a great massage based on the reviews.

I almost fainted when I opened the door. There stood a tall, muscular Greek God of a man who looked exactly like the photos—perfectly sculpted muscular arms, broad shoulders with a tapering waist, and deep eyes that held a magnetic intensity, the whole package. I immediately started to sweat. As I scrambled to pull myself together, he casually walked in and removed his shirt, revealing his flawless physique. I had no idea what was happening. After setting up the massage table, he nonchalantly asked if I preferred a "regular, sensual, or erotic massage." My breath was taken from me. I wasn't anticipating this on the menu for the night. When I finally managed to regain some composure, I blurted out, "Regular."

"Okay," he replied in his strong Eastern European accent, then told me, "Take everything off."

"Everything?" I asked, unsure if I'd heard him right. He simply nodded. "Yes." I left my panties on, hesitated for a moment, and laid down on my stomach. With no cover sheet, I felt incredibly exposed. What on earth did I get myself into?

He poured oil on my back and started kneading it into my shoulders. I relaxed as I submitted to his strong touch. Boy was he amazing! He found every spot that needed attention and never grazed my side boob like the previous creepy masseuse. Although I kind of wanted him too. When he reached my lower back he informed me that he was going to pull my underwear down slightly so he could massage the area properly. My heart skipped a beat. Did he know how bad I wanted him even though I'd said I didn't? I heard him sigh like he was frustrated before telling me that he was just going to take them off completely. Before I knew what was happening my panties were ripped down my legs and thrown to the side. My heart was pounding out of my chest. Was I about to have a happy ending massage? I played it cool as a tornado of desire raged through me.

He continued navigating my body with his magical hands as I lay there butt-ass naked. When he told me to turn on my back I thought for sure he was going to play with me. But he didn't. He went up my thighs until he was an inch away from my lady parts and then moved his hands back down my legs. Was he trying to tease me? I was squirming for him on the inside. He had to know.

Despite it being the best massage I'd ever had, I couldn't help feeling a little disappointed when our session ended without him taking things further.

I flew back home for Christmas the next day still reeling at this close encounter. The missed opportunity consuming my thoughts—so much so that as soon as I touched down in Vegas after my four-week holiday he was the first person I called. I needed him.

The same feelings commenced as soon as he walked through my door. Sweat, overwhelming desire, and slight panic. He had to know what he was doing to me. He still proceeded to ask. "Regular, sensual, or erotic?" I panicked and said, "Regular."

Fuck.

So there I was, lying on my stomach, fully naked this time and kicking myself on the inside. I had waited a month for this and now I was just going to get a regular massage. Great.

He started at my neck and probably heard my screaming thoughts because he asked me again what type of massage I wanted. I grabbed my huge cojones, lifted up my head so that our eyes could meet, and told him I wanted him to fuck me. He said, "Okay, we can do that." I almost fell off the table.

He continued massaging me as my head began to spin. What was he going to do? How was he going to do it? Where were we going to do it? I've never done this before. How was it going to happen?

When he finally got to where I wanted him to be his experienced hands slid between my ass and caressed me skillfully. He gently rubbed around my lady parts until I let out a soft moan. I heard him suck in a breath when he felt how wet I was. And instructed me to turn onto my back. After continuing his gentle massage around my pussy he eased his fingers in and out of me until I felt an unfamiliar feeling.

Before I could think about it for a second longer I squirted all over the place. I have never...done that...in my whole entire life. I didn't even know my body was capable of that. Not once, not twice, but four times! One after the other! The floor was covered in sex juice. My mind was blown.

He took my hand and guided it to his thick, hard penis. I gripped it in my palm and explored downward toward the base. It was below the massage table so I couldn't quite see it as I was lying on my back. So imagine my surprise when my hand just kept going. Not only did this guy look like a God but he had a huge ten-inch megalodon! I had no idea where he thought it was going to fit. He responded to my facial expression with, "It's okay, you can do it." I was living a scene from my wildest dreams.

After he let me revel in his manhood, he moved to the bottom of the table and pulled my hips to meet him. I wrapped my legs around him as he pressed himself inside of my soaking pussy. He moved in slowly until by some miracle he fit it all in. His thrusts were strong and swift. I was in ecstasy. I exclaimed softly that I had no idea what to do with myself and he smirked as he told me not to worry. "I'll do everything." I watched him fuck me for a bit before I touched my clit. I knew I would come immediately and I wanted to savor this beautiful man inside of me for as long as possible. When I reached down to finish I didn't even get two finger circles in before he called me a "good girl," and I let myself go with a scream. He drove into me harder until I was done. He then finished with a satisfying grunt.

Best $300 I ever spent!

A week later I put towels all over my bed so that I could try to make myself squirt like he did. I spent an hour and a copious amount of lube attempting to replicate how he'd touched me, only to finish with the tiniest little dribble—like when you laugh so hard you accidentally let out a drop of pee. Although an underwhelming try, it definitely gave me a good laugh. I guess I was better at other things.

Self-discovery is a lifelong journey— buckle up and enjoy the ride.

Aladdin

For my thirtieth birthday, I decided I wanted to watch the sunrise on Everest. So, I booked a trip to Nepal, filled with excitement and optimism. But let's just say, the mountain had other plans.

Everest Base Camp was the final stop on my fourteen-day trek, perched at 17,598 feet above sea level. While it's high up, this is where climbers begin their journey to the summit of Everest. I wasn't quite that ambitious—I was content with a challenging hike and a breathtaking view.

None of my friends were up for the adventure, so I hired a guide to keep me company and help lead the way. We were seven days in when altitude sickness hit me hard. As I struggled to keep moving, my body decided that this was the perfect moment for my first-ever panic attack. I was convinced I was going to die. It was the most terrifying moment of my life. I somehow made it to our stop for the night, only to be hit by another panic attack when my guide left me alone outside so he could hang out with his friends. My whole world imploded. I spent two hours writing a goodbye letter to my mom as I tried to remind myself how to breathe. By some miracle, I finally managed to drift off to sleep.

When I opened my eyes in the morning, I felt a wave of gratitude like I'd never known before. I honestly thought I wasn't going to make it. At first, I wondered if I was overreacting, but then I looked down at my hands and arms, which were itching uncontrollably. Panic set in as I realized I was having an allergic reaction to the altitude medication. Bumps were spreading across my palms and wrists, and my legs were going numb in random spots. That was it. I was done. I told my guide to get me a helicopter—there was no way I was going any further. It was the hardest, most humbling decision I've ever had to make, but here I am, still alive. And that's what truly matters. No good view is worth your life.

After the disappointing end to my original plan, I was determined to make the most of my additional twenty days in Kathmandu. The locals were welcoming, and the other travelers I met were friendly. Slowly, I was able to put the nightmare from my hike behind me as I immersed myself in the vibrant colors, sights, and sounds of this incredible culture.

I didn't come to Nepal just for Everest—I felt drawn there by its spiritual essence. I sought a deeper knowing of myself and wanted to explore all the various paths to self-awareness. I signed up for sound healing sessions, spa treatments, yoga classes, and meditation workshops, immersing myself in the rich spiritual offerings of the city. I even had a non-happy ending massage at a place that employed people who were visually impaired. It was a profoundly beautiful experience.

Halfway through my trip, I found an all-encompassing retreat for mind, body, and spirit. Without hesitation, I signed up for a twelve-day immersion.

When I arrived, I felt a sense of familiarity, like I knew I was exactly where I needed to be. The tiny two-bedroom, with its broken AC, didn't dampen my mood in the slightest. In fact, I was so open to the experience that I invited a guy I'd matched with on Tinder to join me, free of charge. Although we'd never met in person, our brief conversations on the app and his social media had convinced me he was cool. I figured, why not share the good vibes and see where things might go—I was always open for random romance.

He arrived the next day, and as soon as I laid eyes on him, I knew there was zero chance of me fucking him. He looked better in his photos, and to top it off, he mentioned upon arrival that he was in an open relationship—a detail you're supposed to share upfront. I firmly placed him in the friend zone and made sure not to lead him on in any manner. That said, it was nice to have some company at the retreat, especially since not many people spoke English.

By the third day, as we were finishing lunch, the monkeys that roamed freely around the compound were acting especially bold. They appeared out of nowhere, swiping whole plates of food from unsuspecting diners with lightning speed. While they were undeniably cute, we all knew better than to let our guard down—those monkeys could be dangerous, and a single bite might land you in the hospital. Staying aware of my surroundings had become second nature to me, so I was caught off guard when a guy I hadn't noticed before suddenly struck up a conversation with me in perfect English. Tinder guy had just stepped away to clear his plate, leaving me alone at the table. This Aladdin look-alike bombarded me with quick-fire banter and sharp wit that immediately snapped me out of the slow-paced conversation mode I'd adopted to make communication easier since arriving in the country. He was absolutely hilarious, and I couldn't help but be drawn in.

After laughing until our stomachs hurt for a good ten minutes, we finally settled into the usual "get to know you" questions. He was twenty-three, from London, worked for his dad, and had graduated from a prestigious school just forty-five minutes away from my hometown in the U.S. I couldn't help but wonder if we were somehow destined to meet. While I enjoyed his company, the thought of being with someone so young completely dried up my vagina. I was all too familiar with inexperienced sex, and frankly, I wasn't interested in trying it out again. Still, despite what my lower half was telling me, my upper half absolutely adored this funny, clever guy. So I spent the rest of the day with him laughing and flirting, the chemistry undeniable.

It probably explained why Tinder guy made a hasty exit the next morning. I'm sure he thought he still had a shot until Aladdin waltzed into the picture. Honestly, I was relieved. I was starting to get tired of hearing him snore all night anyway.

The moment Aladdin caught wind of Tinder guy's departure, he laid on the full press. I was showered with his undivided attention and affection at every turn. It felt so good to be courted properly.

My favorite moments with him were during the guided meditations. He always made a point to sit next to me, subtly translating the speaker's foreign language into English, but with a twist—he'd occasionally whisper hilarious, made-up translations just for me. "When everyone falls silent, you have to shout 'MOO' as loud as you can," he'd mutter, his eyes twinkling with mischief. I struggled to keep a straight face in the otherwise solemn atmosphere, my body shaking with suppressed laughter in a way I'd never experienced with anyone else.

As much as I enjoyed his company, I couldn't shake my skepticism about taking things to the next level. I didn't want to risk having disappointing sex or, worse, ruining the friendship that had quickly become something I valued.

On the sixth day, he insisted I follow him to his room to "see the view." Intrigued by the promise of a good sight, I went along. However, the lack of any notable view quickly made it clear that his intentions were far from innocent. By the time I realized it, he was already leaning in to kiss me. I reciprocated for a moment, but pulled away shortly after. I still wasn't sexually interested, and frankly, his body odor was pungent in the sweltering Nepal heat. I came up with a quick excuse to leave, hoping he'd take the hint and let things end there.

I didn't see him for the rest of the day so I went back to his room so we could walk to the evening meditation together. I entered as he was getting out of the shower. He smelled delicious and let his towel drop to reveal his semi-hard penis. As I was admiring the view he quickly informed me that it got bigger. Although the comment was unnecessary, I became a little aroused at the thought of his already good-sized member growing larger than it was.

Even so, I stood my ground and instructed him to get dressed so that we wouldn't miss our meditation. He pushed for us to skip it and lay together, but I had to explain that I wasn't interested in having sex with someone as young as him. I tried to make him understand that there's a way an experienced man makes love that cannot be replicated by an inexperienced boy. And I knew that this would be the case with him, so I thought it would be best to just be friends. But he wouldn't let it go and assured me that it wouldn't be like that until I finally decided, why not? We were in the middle of the Nepalese jungle and I was here to experience. So why not experience it fully? I loved being around him and it had been six months since the last time I saw a penis. I convinced myself that he couldn't be that bad. My famous last words.

We lay on his bed while making out. His kisses were passionate yet desperate for more. I was so excited to have sex that I looked past the part where he didn't hold me like I wanted to be held. Or kiss me all over. Or caress me. Or appreciate my body like my previous good lovers. He didn't even take off my shirt. As we were almost at the sex part he had the audacity to ask me for a blowjob while refusing to eat me out. Uhm, no. Absolutely not. I knew it was going to be like this so I couldn't even be mad.

He entered me and started to thrust. No touching, no kissing, no variation of speed. Just him, in and out of me at a constant quick rate, in missionary. It wasn't bad, but it wasn't great. I touched myself as he held off from finishing until I was ready. At least he'd gotten that part right. We orgasmed together while our moans echoed through the opened window. I'm sure everyone in the vicinity heard.

I lay there partially satisfied by this subpar experience that went exactly how I'd predicted it would. And it did not get bigger. Why must boys lie? Since we were friends before playmates I figured I could show him how to make love to a woman properly the next time. For now, I was happy to lay in his arms. When he got up to go to the bathroom he turned to me and asked me proudly how it was. I wasn't sure who this guy usually had sex with but it obviously wasn't with people who told the truth. I replied "Meh," and rolled over to sleep.

He didn't talk to me for two days after that.

Apparently, WitMaster 5000 had a huge and fragile ego that I had completely decimated with my tiny little "meh." Looking back, I could see how harsh it sounded, but that was the truth. It was just *boom boom, done.* The concept that sex is more than a penis being jabbed in and out of a woman is not usually grasped by younger lovers. I warned him and I wasn't about to lie. Sorry, not sorry.

That being said, I had grown to like him as more than just a friend, so I made an effort to keep talking to him, even though he insisted on being distant and upset.

Once I thawed him out of his icy demeanor he invited me back to his place. It was annoying how long it took to charm him.

We ended up in his bed, falling into the same rhythm as before. It all happened so quickly that I didn't want to pause and give him a lesson. I kept my thoughts to myself as he gently caressed me to sleep afterward. I hadn't realized how much I missed being in someone's arms until I was in his. All he needed to do was channel the same tenderness he showed me into foreplay and his sex game. It wasn't difficult—he was a caring person, just a little inexperienced when it came to intimacy.

The next day, he was back to who he was pre-sex—until I suggested I could show him how I liked to be touched. He rudely brushed me off. The chorus from Katy Perry's "Hot N Cold" song was definitely his anthem.

We ended up in his shower at the end of the night. He pinned me against the wall with his hips as the water trickled around us. He placed one steadying hand above me and the other behind my neck. Pulling me up to meet his lips. I could feel his heart with my chest as our soaking bodies pressed together. He explored my neck with his mouth and then lifted me up by my ass so that our faces were level. He was a good kisser and the fact that he was actually trying really turned me on. I decided I would bless him with a blowjob. I knew the favor wasn't going to be returned but I knew it was because he didn't know how to do it and was scared of hearing another "meh." I went down on my knees and started to pleasure him. He almost came immediately so we had to stop and move to the bed to finish up.

The age difference was a distant memory as I lay in his arms. My last five days in Nepal were filled with inner peace and Aladdin. He made up for not knowing how to fuck me properly by cuddling me to sleep every night. It was a trade-off I was more than happy to accept.

As I packed my things, I couldn't help but wonder what our goodbye would be like. Would we share a lingering look of sadness? Embrace tightly, not wanting to let go? Make plans to see each other again? Or would he try to convince me to stay?

I heard a knock on my door and knew it was him. Taking a deep breath, I walked over and opened it, but found no one there. Looking out the window, I saw him walking away without looking back. That damn asshole didn't even say goodbye to me.

I hopped into the cab and found solace in the fact that it was his loss. No point in having a dramatic goodbye with someone you'll never see again anyway.

Two hours later, he messaged me, claiming he'd come to my door but no one had answered. I wanted to unleash everything I was feeling, but I knew he wasn't mature enough to handle it. So, I settled for a simple thumbs-up emoji and moved on with my life. He was nothing more than a nice thing of the past.

Or so I thought.

Apparently, he didn't think he'd done anything wrong, as he kept sending me memes on social media every few days. I ignored them for the first month, then responded sarcastically the next, but he just kept going. Eventually, I realized it was time to let go of any lingering resentment. He had been my favorite part of Nepal, and holding onto a grudge no longer made any sense.

Three years later, after countless memes and messages exchanged, I decided to plan a trip to the UK. My first stop was London to "visit friends"—though, unbeknownst to anyone, mostly him. When he invited me to stay at his place, all the feelings I'd kept buried came rushing back. But I knew I had to decline. I didn't want to impose or rush into anything physical. I had been celibate since we were last together, and I wasn't about to break that vow unless I felt it would be truly worth it. Plus, we'd planned a four-day road trip together, and I thought holding off on intimacy would give us the space to reconnect and appreciate each other even more.

As my departure drew closer, I found myself dreaming about him, filled with excitement and anticipation. I couldn't wait to join him at the luxurious spots he often posted about on social media. He was wealthy, a regular at exclusive clubs and upscale parties, and I was eager to show him a different side of me—one polished and dressed up for a night out. After all, the only version he'd ever seen was the sweaty, hippie traveler I'd been in Nepal.

The plane ride was excruciating as I anxiously counted down the minutes until touchdown. My heart was fluttering as I checked into my hotel so I could quickly shower. He was on his way and I was over the moon. When I got the message that he'd arrived, I practically flew downstairs.

There he was, standing in the lobby, patiently waiting for me. Before I even had time to think, I ran to him and threw myself into his arms. I was overwhelmed with joy as he picked me up and held me. It felt like one of those emotional videos you stumble upon at 2 a.m. when you should be sleeping. We stood there, wrapped in each other's embrace, lost in the moment, completely unaware of the awkward glances from the reception staff. I never wanted to let go. I had missed him more than I could have ever imagined.

As we stepped outside the hotel, he looked down at me with his gentle brown eyes and kissed me. His lips were inviting, but I held back. I wanted more than just a fleeting kiss—I wanted to spend time together, to go out and be courted the way any thirty-three-year-old woman deserves.

I kissed him back anyway as I my insides protested.

It took all my willpower to pull myself away from his face, but I knew I had to. I wanted to take things slow. I suggested we go for the walk we had originally planned, and he took my hand and led me toward the park across the street, stopping every few minutes to kiss me.

When we found a spot to sit, he couldn't keep his hands off me, excitedly proclaiming how much he loved PDAs. It felt like we were long-lost lovers, reunited after years apart—and I couldn't deny, I *wanted* this. But just as quickly as those sweet moments blossomed, they were interrupted by his constant insistence that we go back to his place. I wasn't ready for that. I wasn't interested in just rushing into sex. I knew that the moments leading up to intimacy made the act even better. He was treating it like it didn't matter.

After my failed attempts to have a conversation around his constant kisses, I suggested we head to a bar. I assumed he'd have some upscale spot in mind, given how often he seemed to frequent them. But he didn't. We ended up at the first bar that popped up on Google Maps.

I was thoroughly underwhelmed. The bar was dull and nearly empty. We ordered basic drinks and sat there for twenty minutes while he fidgeted with his Patek watch until he was sure I noticed it and complained about having to hang out with his billionaire friend who was in town. He was trying to flaunt his wealth to impress me and it was giving me the ick. Besides, if he didn't want to spend time with someone, why make plans to do so? I was starting to realize he hadn't matured the way I'd hoped. Slowly, I sipped my second drink, trying to prolong the inevitable.

When I'd finally had enough of his complaining, I agreed to go to his house. As we walked hand in hand to his drop-top Bentley he excitedly mentioned that I could meet his mom, as if that would somehow make me more thrilled to go. He was so confusing. This guy didn't want to take me out before fucking me, but now insisted I meet his mom? Why?

He held my hand as we cruised through the unfamiliar streets in his expensive car, his posture straightening with each admiring glance from passersby. It was painfully obvious that he thrived off the validation of strangers. It was such small dick energy.

The houses started getting bigger as we got closer to his. I wondered what his net worth was. When we first met in Nepal, I knew his family was well-off, but I never imagined him to be *rich* rich. Regardless of my profession, his money didn't make me like him more or less. It was just a bonus to how I already felt about him minus a couple of icks.

As we pulled into the driveway of his parents' mansion, he paused and asked if I wanted to see the new house he'd just bought before we went inside. I was one thousand percent down. I loved sharing the excitement of a new home purchase with my friends.

We drove around the corner to an even bigger home.

He led me through his new place with a childlike enthusiasm, keeping me close as I admired each room and showering me with kisses as if he couldn't get enough.

After the tour, he put on some music and casually asked, "Do you like champagne? Only the good stuff, of course."

He directed me to open the fridge, where a brand-new bottle of Dom Perignon sparkled back at me. I could see his ego grow as he watched my reaction. I was impressed that he had my favorite champagne on deck, yet given his car and mansion, I expected nothing less. We started drinking and dancing, just like when we first met. I finally felt relaxed, enjoying the fun I'd been hoping for with him. Still, deep down, I knew this was the bare minimum compared to the night out I wanted.

We ended up at his parents' place shortly after. He handed me the open bottle of champagne and led me to meet his mom. It wasn't the classy first impression I'd hoped for, but he seemed completely unfazed. His mom was incredibly sweet, but between the alcohol and the jet lag, I felt a wave of nervousness and couldn't think of a single thing to say when he left me alone with her. I'd never been rendered speechless before, and I was not a fan of the feeling.

After what felt like an eternity, he finally rescued me from my discomfort by summoning me away. I followed him through a maze of corridors, eventually arriving at a completely separate wing of the house. There, he had a spacious apartment within his parents' grand estate. It was impressive, but the mess was hard to ignore. Despite having housekeepers and maids at his disposal, there was no effort to keep it presentable. Beside his bed, I spotted an empty bottle of Don Julio 1942—a bottle I knew he hadn't consumed alone. I was pretty disappointed. It was as if he'd had a party with someone else just hours before meeting up with me. Smooth.

He walked over to the window and gestured for me to come see the "amazing view." I eagerly skipped over, only to realize it was just another mediocre ploy to get me closer to his bed—exactly like in Nepal. Had he really not come up with a new move since then? I was obviously the dumb one who kept falling for it.

I clutched my champagne glass and insisted he wait until I finished. As much as I wanted to be with him, I wasn't sure I was ready. It had been a long time since I'd been with him—or anyone, for that matter. I didn't think he understood that. This wasn't how I had imagined it in my head, but as I emptied my glass, I convinced myself we could do the things I had pictured afterward—like go to a nice dinner, dance at a nightclub, and take our road trip.

So there we were, on his bed, tasting the champagne on each other's lips. I succumbed to his tenacity and I was all in for a sexy time. He hastily pulled down my pink underwear and started to eat me out. It was pretty decent until he pressed his closed mouth face onto my clit and shook his head back and forth, forcing me to feel the bristles on his cheeks. I wanted to find out which porno did this so I could erase it from existence. Not sexy.

We finally got to the sex part and it was the same amateur motions that I had experienced three years prior. All *boom boom*, no passion. In the middle of banging me he asked if I was ready to come. "Maybe if you slowed down like I asked, Mr. Jackhammer," I almost snapped back but refrained as I remembered his sensitive ego. I touched myself hastily so we could finish together.

Other than his almost good cunnilingus skills, nothing had changed. The mediocre sex was forgotten as soon as I was in his arms afterward, just like Nepal.

We lay there while he went on about having to meet up with his billionaire friend again. I had expected to spend the entire night with him, especially after he'd been all over me all day, so I was pretty confused when he only half-heartedly invited me. I could not fathom the idea of being fucked and dumped so I colored that red flag green and got up to get ready.

We both showered while his chef drilled straw holes in coconuts, so we could sip the juice on our way to the restaurant. What a life. We held each other, cradling our drinks the whole Uber ride there. I asked if we could swing by my hotel so I could change, but he insisted there wasn't enough time. I smiled to myself, remembering that we were running late because I had been lying in his arms. It made me think about our road trip plans, so I brought it up—but he quickly brushed it off, changing the subject entirely. This time I didn't color the flag.

We met up with his friend at a restaurant, where he was already seated with three other girls. The music was so loud it made conversation nearly impossible, so I retreated into my own world as I sipped on more expensive champagne. I wasn't in the mood for a shouting match. I placed my hand on Aladdin's thigh to let him know I was still with him, even though I wasn't being social, but there was no reciprocal touch like there had been the whole afternoon. That stung, especially coming from someone who'd been all about PDAs.

To make the whole situation worse, he casually leaned in and whispered that his friend wanted to go to a venue with a dress code, and told him that I wasn't dressed up enough. Well, no fucking shit—I was still in the same outfit I'd worn for our afternoon walk. If you've been to London, you know there's no way you're getting into any upscale place underdressed. The doormen would size you up and deny entry with a look that would make you feel like the scum of the earth. Seeing my expression, Aladdin assured me he'd convince his friend to go somewhere everyone could get in. Which, honestly, should've been the first thing he did before saying anything. I knew deep down I was being ding dong ditched.

My suspicions were confirmed after just five minutes of them whispering in each other's ears. He turned to me and said they'd decided to go to the place with the dress code. I was right. I was not welcomed and I needed to get out of there as fast as possible.

To say I was angry was an understatement. I saw red. This boy had literally spent the whole day complaining about his friend while trying to fuck me, and now, after he got what he wanted, was trying to get rid of me for his friend. I wanted to crawl out of my own skin. Honestly, I almost ran straight to the airport. He walked me to the exit and kissed me goodbye like nothing had changed. Then he asked if he'd see me tomorrow, and I shot back a sarcastic "yeah," fully knowing I'd rather drink bleach than ever speak to him again. All I felt was rage—toward him, and toward myself for ever believing there was something special between us.

I headed to another bar, met some incredible people, and ended up getting completely wasted with them. Screw him.

At 3 in the morning, he messaged me to ask if I was still upset. When I left his message on read, he added that there were no girls around him, it was just him and his friend, and that he wasn't responsible for the dress code. The fury inside me rose again. This guy was out to lunch. The last thing I cared about was whether or not he was hanging out with other girls. This wasn't a teen drama—this was about respect, and he was completely oblivious to it. I was just going to continue ignoring him but my intoxicated fingers told him to fuck right off as I proceeded with the awesome night I was having.

The next morning hit like every brutal hangover—head pounding, regret hanging in the air. As I tried to piece together the events of the previous day, a heavy sense of doom settled over me. It was that hollow feeling, like the moment you realize someone you cared about is gone—and won't ever be coming back. I was devastated, and for the life of me, I couldn't understand why. Was I actually mourning the loss of this superficial, entitled jerk, who was so far up his wealthier friend's ass that he had no sense of reality?

I sat with the emptiness for a few moments, and then it hit me, hard. I had been in love with him, all along. From Nepal—the sound of his voice, his humor, his intelligence, his laugh, the way his eyes lit up. The quiet confidence he carried as he walked. How I felt when he held me. How had I missed it? How did I not know?

I needed to talk to him again. Maybe he didn't fully realize what he'd done. He was more self-aware than most people, so I figured he'd be open to clearing the air.

Boy, was I wrong. He sent my call straight to voicemail and ignored my text. It felt like a replay of Nepal, when he'd ghosted me for two days because I "meh'd" him. This time, though, I didn't have two days to wait. I had to see him before I left.

I sent another message with a more detailed explanation about the situation, and he dismissed my words by telling me, "I showed you nothing but kindness, and you took everything the wrong way. I thought you were more mature than that."

Ouch.

This, my friends, is what gaslighting looks like. This boy called *me* immature and was trying to make *me* feel like an idiot for feeling upset at being fucked and dumped. What a complete piece of shit.

I didn't want to be done with him, but I knew I had no choice. The only thing left unfinished was my favorite shirt, which I'd left at his place. When he ignored my request to drop it off, I let him know I'd be stopping by the day before I left to pick it up. So much for that road trip.

As much as I was angry with him, I still hoped that we could salvage our friendship. It was clear that we were definitely not romantically compatible. On my way to his place, I picked up a hanging plant as a peace offering and housewarming gift. He'd been so proud showing me around his new place, and it was a tradition of mine to gift my friends their first plant for their first home. When I arrived at his door, I set it aside. I wanted to invite him on a walk without him feeling obligated by a gift.

He opened the door with an attitude and exclaimed, "Ah, me and my archnemesis meet again." What was wrong with this child?

I pulled him in for a hug and asked if he'd like to join me for a quick stroll. He declined, saying he was tired and wanted to take a nap. I hid my disappointment and offered again, but this time, his refusal came with a scrunched-up face and an irritated tone.

I don't know what made me think I would get any response other than this. I had to get out of there ASAP. I mentioned I had a gift for him while grabbing the plant from the side. He looked flabbergasted when I placed it into his hands. I wanted to bask in the surprise element that I usually loved, but felt nothing. He spewed out a bunch of nonsense in attempts to make me laugh but I was too numb to comprehend any of it.

I turned around and walked away without looking back.

I ended up in a secluded area surrounded by trees in the nearby nature reserve and sat there in silence for hours, hoping a reconnection with Mother Earth would ease my aching heart. I was crushed. How could I be so stupid, *again*? Didn't I have enough life experience to read the signs? Was I simply a glutton for punishment? I was furious with myself for having a silly dream of a silly boy.

The only comfort I found was remembering the plant I bought him: *Epipremnum aureum*, also known as pothos. Specifically chosen because it's nearly indestructible. So after I am long gone and over him he will still have something that reminds him of me. Petty, I know, but great for comedic effect.

When someone shows you who they are, believe them. There are so many things that are more important than a person who doesn't want you.

Myself

The last person I loved should've been the first. Myself. I spent years running away from me—letting the pain of past failures and heartaches cloud my judgment. I let loneliness mislead me into the arms of people who didn't deserve a second of my time. The act of intimacy was used as a band-aid for wounds I wasn't ready to face. But all it did was magnify the void, because love isn't something you can extract from someone else to fill you. It has to come from within.

It took a long time for me to understand that sex isn't a healing balm. It isn't an escape. It's meant to be sacred. Special. A celebration of connection, not an act of convenience or method of numbing.

I say this with conviction: My inner peace is worth more than any approval or validation. Any situation or person can be left at any time, without an explanation. "No" is a complete sentence. And no one is allowed to coerce me into anything I don't want to do. Those who don't respect that don't deserve a place in my life. I'd rather be alone than ill-accompanied.

I'm grateful for all the participants in my dating era and the lessons they came with—good and bad. I am a passionate and wild (like the flower) woman who loves fiercely. Some will never appreciate or value that, because people can only meet you at the depth at which they've met themselves. And from here on out, I will never lower my standards for potential.

Every rejection is a divine redirection. Trust that what's meant for you will never miss you.

It wasn't easy to stand where I am. It definitely wasn't always kind. I've been loved, used, hurt, the hurter, and everything in between. I forgive them all. But more importantly, I forgive myself—for ignoring the quiet whispers of my intuition and for not prioritizing myself when I needed to the most.

My memories now serve as wisdom, not wounds.

I am the Disney savior of my story. My own happily ever after.

MYSELF

The most important relationship you will ever have is the one with yourself. So always, always, always love yourself first.

 : @thenellanovella

www.ingramcontent.com/pod-product-compliance
Lightning Source LLC
LaVergne TN
LVHW041924070526
838199LV00051BA/2713